Crucial Study Texts for Computing Degree Courses

Titles in the series

Computer Networks	ISBN: 1 90337 06 2	Price £12.00
Computer Systems Architecture	ISBN: 1 90337 07 0	Price £10.00
Databases	ISBN: 1 90337 08 9	Price £12.00
Multimedia Computing	ISBN: 1 90337 18 6	Price £12.00
User Interface Design	ISBN: 1 90337 19 4	Price £12.00
Visual Programming	ISBN: 1 90337 11 9	Price £12.00

To order, please call our order line 0845 230 9000, or email orders@learningmaters.co.uk, or visit our website www.learningmatters.co.uk

Databases

R. L. Warrender

Computing series editor:
Peter Hodson

First published in 2003 by Crucial, a division of Learning Matters Ltd.

British Library Cataloguing in Publication Data
A CIP record for this book is available from the British Library

ISBN 1 903337 08 9

Cover design by Topics – The Creative Partnership
Project management by Deer Park Productions
Text design by Code 5 Design
Typeset by TW Typesetting, Plymouth, Devon
Printed and bound by Bell & Bain Ltd, Glasgow

Learning Matters Ltd
33 Southernhay East
Exeter EX1 1NX
Tel: 01392 215560
Email: info@learningmatters.co.uk
www.learningmatters.co.uk

Contents

Foreword

This may seem like just another book which introduces the concepts of databases, but this book is much more than that. Most books which attempt to introduce databases also tend to cover more detailed topics, and thus can become too lengthy and in-depth for an introductory reader. This book, being a study text, does the job of informing the target audience of the concepts that they need to learn to develop and manage database systems into much better practice. The fact that it is concise and uses a large number of examples and exercises, with solutions and explanations, aids in developing introductory understanding. It also gives pointers to other sources of information so that the reader can always further examine more advanced concepts in depth.

This makes this book ideal for its target audience, where it is aimed at HND, foundation level and undergraduate level courses in computing and information technology. At this level, students expect to gain an understanding of database concepts, both the theoretical underpinning of how to design database systems, but also a practical understanding of how to use one of the most popular database systems used in teaching nowadays, Access. A student reading this book will have experience in all areas of database systems which are necessary in academia and industry, from understanding the most popular relational data model to design issues such as using the ER modelling tool and normalisation to correctly produce industrial strength databases. Other important concepts such as security, concurrency and transaction management are also covered in a way that a student can gain basic understanding. Practical issues take the student through a set of exercises to begin to use the Access database system, as well as how to design forms and how to use the SQL query language to perform a large number of basic to fairly complex queries. The book then finally introduces some of the more advanced areas of database systems, including the highly popular area of web database systems and distributed systems, and then discusses some of the newer trends, specifically newer data models other than relational, and XML. These are all areas which should be included in any introductory database systems course.

This book also has a wider appeal in that anybody wishing to gain an understanding of important database concepts would hugely benefit from reading it. It would also do well as a revision aid or as a source of reference at all levels.

Dr David Nelson
Senior Lecturer
University of Sunderland

Preface

The object of this Study Text is to introduce you to the world of computer databases and is intended for students studying HND, Foundation degrees as well as conventional degree courses in Computing and Information Technology. We will examine the many questions which can be asked in an exam context as well as explore the practicalities of hands-on machine-based activities. A good thorough grounding in database principles will aid your conceptual understanding in many areas such as information systems and data management. Having the ability to manipulate as well as collect meaningful data is a very practical skill and one that is now expected by industry.

First we need to discuss some important terminology. Databases are in effect collections of data. Data are pieces of information we feel are important enough to store for future reference. Database management systems (DBMS) are the programs designed to manipulate data within a database – in particular to ensure the overall integrity of the data within the database. The role of the database management system cannot be stressed too highly. These are the routines for accessing and storing data within the database.

Two of the most popular DBMS within an educational environment are Access and Oracle. Oracle is a client/server object-relational DBMS commonly used in business for high-end database applications. Although Microsoft also has a similar high-end relational client/server product (SQL Server), by including Microsoft Access as part of its Office Suite, Microsoft have created a large installed base for its product and is arguably the preferred choice for many small and medium size enterprises (SMEs). Access is a relational database management system (RDBMS). We have therefore based the examples contained within the book on Microsoft Access but have included some information related to the differences between Oracle and Access. These primarily relate to 'dialect' differences in the structured query language (SQL) as well as some notes on using client/server architecture.

It is important when you are studying databases to firmly grasp the concepts as you go along. Do not put matters to one side and expect that one day you will receive some sudden understanding after which the whole subject will become instantly clear. Much of the subject builds on a foundation of concepts. Practical tutorials help reinforce ideas and should not be avoided.

If you are having any difficulty in grasping any of the concepts, then talk with your lecturer or tutor on this matter. Although this Study Text takes you through the essentials of databases, this is no reason to skip classes. While attending classes does not guarantee a pass, we often comment on the fact that there is a strong correlation between students who do not attend classes and those who fail exams.

Within the context of a school environment, pupils are expected to attend school for a certain number of hours each week. In the UK (as in many other countries) if parents fail to send their children to school, they are likely to face legal prosecution under the law. In addition to attendance, pupils generally receive a quantity of homework that will be monitored by school staff. Failure to carryout the prescribed homework normally would result in loss of privileges or other form of punishment.

At further and higher education establishments the situation is completely different. Responsibility for your education passes over to yourself as a recognised adult. Courses are divided into academic years and semesters which in turn are divided into course modules appropriate to your chosen area of study. Each module will carry a certain level of 'credit' which equates to a suitable 'learning time'.

For example:

Code	Title	Level	Credits	Learning time
COM220	Database Systems Development	2	20	200

In this case we have a Level 2 Database module with a suggested learning time of 200 hours. In reality, the total 'contact time' may be as little as 2 hours per week over perhaps only 24 teaching weeks. The term 'contact time' refers to formal time given to a student either as a lecture, tutorial, lab session, workshop, etc. For the above module this may only total up to $24 \times 2 = 48$ hours over the course of an academic year.

Simply put, a student should be capable of passing this module based on 48 hours of attendance supplemented with up to a total of 152 hours of directed study in their own time. A modern student has to be self-motivated and diligent, putting in many hours of private study to ensure adequate knowledge of the subject. How many hours you put in per week clearly will vary from student to student. A great deal depends on prior knowledge and experience, particularly in the earlier levels, but also on your own natural ability to understand the subject. Certainly you should not be ashamed to study – most degrees and higher diplomas are earned not so much by super-intelligent individuals but by those who can organise themselves systematically and for whom studying becomes a way of life rather than a 'drag'.

Finally get to know your library as well as the Internet. The Internet is a wonderful tool where a great deal of valuable information can be obtained in a short time. However, it is also largely unregulated, meaning that much of what you read may be opinion rather than fact. You academic institution library facility should have copies of all directed reading as well as other books on your subject. They also have access to a wide range of peer-reviewed journals and papers in your subject area. By all means supplement this with web searches, particularly in areas where you have access to a growing number of academic digital libraries such as ACM, IEEE, Citeseer, etc. However, be careful about referencing information taken from unregulated sites as it may in fact be totally erroneous.

Acknowledgements

Books are rarely the work of one individual and in that context I would like to acknowledge those behind the scenes who directly contributed to the success of this project.

First, my long-suffering wife Denise and daughter Jennifer who put up with my many late-night sessions and still wonder why I can't just be 'normal'. Denise helped with the initial proofreading with Jennifer testing out some of the tutorials.

To Mandy Preece and Jonathan Harris at Learning Matters Ltd as well as the series editor Peter Hodson who have shown considerable faith in bringing the book to publication.

To Phil Irving for getting me involved in this project and Sue Stirk whose work formed the basis for the SQL Tutorial.

And last but not least to my friend and colleague David Nelson for the time taken to review the technical content of the book and the helpful suggestions offered for improvements in many areas.

R. L. Warrender,
Senior Lecturer
University of Sunderland

Chapter 1
Introduction to databases and DBMS

Chapter summary

This introduction looks at the origins of databases using conventional file storage techniques through to the modern-day use of database management systems (DBMS). It examines such aspects as the separation of data definition from individual application programs in favour of creating a common database management system containing detailed descriptions of the data it holds. This facilitates a much more robust software system capable of sharing data and avoiding data duplication.

The text looks at two of the early data models, namely hierarchical and network models, before describing the most common model in use today, namely the relational data model.

Learning outcomes

After studying this chapter, you should check your knowledge against the outcomes below and test your achievement by answering the questions at the end of the chapter. You should be able to:

Outcome 1: Understand the evolution from file storage through to DBMS.
It is important to see how inventions such as magnetic disk drives changed significantly the process of modelling real-world information and data. You should be able to describe this evolutional change.

Outcome 2: Understand the separation of data definition from applications.
As multi-user systems developed, storing of data definition within individual applications can result in data contention and inconsistency. You should be able to describe how separating the data definition from applications and holding this in a DBMS allows applications to request items of data, leaving the DBMS to figure out how to retrieve, unpack and deliver this data.

Outcome 3: Appreciate the development of data models over time.
Although industry has standardised on relational databases, the time period over which these changes took place still means that a great deal of legacy data exists in other database formats. You should be able to appreciate the issue of legacy data as well as discuss ways of using this. Understanding previous data models is clearly an important first step.

Outcome 4: Understand the basis of the relational data model.
A great deal more will be said in later chapters – for the present it is important to understand and be able to answer questions on both the basis of the relational model as well as much of its terminology.

How will you be assessed on this?

This chapter serves as an introduction to database systems. It blends historical information with some key concepts that most definitely will be assessed. Look out for these definitions and important concepts within this section. You will also require a working knowledge concerning the evolution of the modern-day DBMS system. Generally questions on this section will be short and to the point.

Section 1

Defining a database

CRUCIAL CONCEPT

A **database** is essentially a means of storage and retrieval of items of data. The data is usually either numerical or textual, although other data forms can be accommodated.

Databases have been around much longer than the modern computer although the term database did not come into common usage until the 1960s, some time after the invention of the magnetic disk. Data had previously been stored on punched cards or paper tapes, and used with a variety of mechanical devices. One such early application was Herman Hollerith's tabulating and sorting machine invented in 1890 to automate the process of the US census, a process that would have taken eight years but was reduced by automation to only two and a half years.

Clearly storage of data existed even long before this time but whether you would term these databases depends on how loose you make your definition and whether you regard sorting, querying and overwriting a necessary prerequisite. Certainly today no database would be complete without such facilities, with data being referred to as 'persistent' giving it the characteristic of being ready and available when required.

The need for a database

Since the advent of electronic computers together with magnetic hard drives, database technology has become a very important aspect of business systems.

CRUCIAL CONCEPT

Virtually all computer programs require a means of storage of **persistent data**, i.e. data that will be available the next time the program will run or indeed when the computer is switched on.

Accounting programs need to save details of financial transactions; university or college record systems need to store details of students' marks. Programs need to be able to build on past information rather than only process current or new data. Also data from previous sessions needs to be available in its complete form (not just as totals) to permit detailed analysis.

Initially data was saved in the form of records, often on punched cards or magnetic tape drives. However, this changed quite dramatically with the invention of the magnetic disk drive (or hard drive) in the 1950s allowing random data access instead of serial data access.

For a while programs continued to save data in the form of records mimicking the serial data device approach. For example, a typical record for, say, a personal music collection could have been:

CD no.	4 digits
Song title	40 characters
Artiste	35 characters
Chart position	1 digit
Month	2 digits
Year	4 digits

A program could then be written to access this stored data and print an updated list by artiste's name. To do this, the program would need to read the file, record by record, until it had the necessary information to produce the required output.

If the stored data was already known to be in the correct order, then clearly it would read one record and print the result before proceeding with the next record. However, if some sorting of the records were required, then this would likely be done in two passes, the first pass to determine the required order of the records with a second pass to retrieve the next record for printing. In the above example, with a fixed record size of 86 characters (a digit being a type of character), the 32nd record would be located some $32 \times 86 = 2,752$ characters from the start of the file. While this is possible with hard drive technology, it does highlight the difficulty in using such media as punched cards or magnetic tape drives where random access is not possible.

Problems in applications directly accessing a file database

Storing data as fixed length records using the operating system's file storage facilities had several disadvantages:

- Details of the file record had to be part of the application program. If the record format changed, then all programs using the records also had to be changed. In addition, a program had to be written to read each existing record and store it in a new file in its changed format.
- Because data was developed for a given application, it often resulted in the same information residing in two different files. Not only is this a waste of effort, it also could lead to problems of inconsistency between different applications.
- Attempts at trying to share data between applications invariably led to the need to change the record format, in turn causing problems listed above.

Quick test

Define what we mean by 'persistent data' and give some examples of where this is required.

Section 2

The DBMS approach

What was required was a way of taking the data definition out of the applications program and placing this along with the data within its own interface, namely a database management system (DBMS).

─────── CRUCIAL CONCEPT ───────

The **DBMS** would not only be responsible for all database activities (storage, retrieval, indexing, etc.), but also be responsible for keeping a detailed description of the data being held. This is referred to as 'meta-data', i.e. data (or information) about the data being held. It is also sometimes referred to as the **schema** or alternatively as the **data dictionary**.

Figure 1.1 diagrammatically shows the separation of database storage from the user or application interface. The schema or data dictionary stores all necessary information about the individual fields, allowing the applications to access individual data items by simply passing the request over to the DBMS. Knowing the structure of the data, the DBMS is able to locate and unpack the data, passing this back to the calling program. This leads to more robust programming, more scope for data sharing and less data duplication.

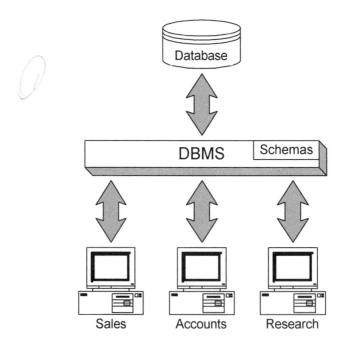

Figure 1.1 DBMS showing interface with three typical applications

Early implementations of DBMS occurred in the 1960s using the hierarchical and network data models. Although some legacy systems and data still exist, new systems now almost exclusively utilise DBMS based on the relational data model (or some later derivation – this will be discussed in Chapter 11).

Hierarchical data model

The hierarchical data model was arranged on a top-down structure resembling an inverted tree (see Figure 1.2). It uses the concept of *parent* and *child* to describe its structure. Implicit in its definition is that a child could only be related to one parent.

Network data model

The network data model was in fact a more general representation of the hierarchical data model with no distinction being made between parent and child.

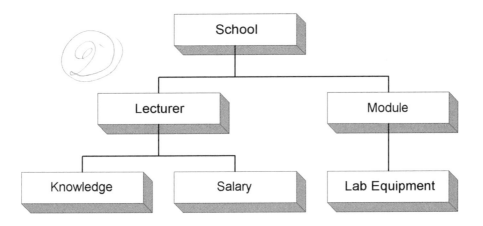

Figure 1.2 Hierarchical database model

In the example shown in Figure 1.3 note that Lab Equipment is associated with both a Module as well as a Lecturer record data. The arrows indicate plurality in that there can be several pieces of equipment required for a module. Similarly, a lecturer may require several pieces of equipment.

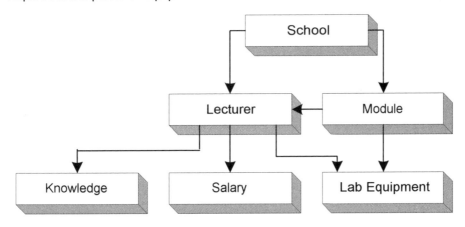

Figure 1.3 Network database model

Quick test

Why is it preferable to separate database storage from the user or application interface?

Section 3

Relational data model

The relational data model first appeared in the early 1970s mainly due to the efforts of E. F. Codd, a mathematician who studied at Oxford and joined IBM in 1949. Codd wanted to take the responsibility of finding and controlling information away from the user and provide an interface which would accept simple appropriate commands to find whatever was needed.

Relational databases represent their data as collections of two-dimensional tables. The columns represent fields within a record and the rows represent individual records. Taking the example cited previously, we could represent our mythical CD collection as in Table 1.1.

Table 1.1 CD table

CD no.	Song	Artiste	Position	Month	Year
0001	Woman	John Lennon	1	02	1981
0002	Make Your Mind Up	Bucks Fizz	2	04	1981
0003	You Can't Hurry Love	Phil Collins	11	02	1983
0004	It's a Hard Life	Queen	9	07	1984
0005	A Kind of Magic	Queen	5	04	1985
0006	Toy Boy	Sinitta	6	09	1987
0007	You Got It	Roy Orbison	4	02	1989

─── CRUCIAL CONCEPT ───

While the terms **tables**, **columns** and **rows** are in common usage, their mathematical or formal names are as follows:

table	–	**relation** (or **entity type**)
column	–	**attribute** (or **field**)
row	–	**tuple** (or **record**)

While this could represent a very simple database of a CD collection, let us examine what happens in the real world where there could be more relations to add to the database. Consider that we may want to keep track of who we lend the CDs out to – imagine this is a CD library where we have many customers borrowing CDs on an irregular basis. First we may want to store information on our customers as in Table 1.2.

Table 1.2 Customer table

Cust. no.	Name	Address
001	James Burke	125 West High Street, Fulham
002	Heather Young	12 Old Mill Lane, Derby
003	Robert Walker	63 Shaw Park Drive, Glasgow
004	Jean Mackie	13 Durham Lane, Sheffield
005	Paul Mackie	13 Durham Lane, Sheffield
006	Cedric Thomas	22 Willows Gardens, Cardiff
007	Ian Leslie	23 Ardennes Terrace, Belfast

─── CRUCIAL CONCEPT ───

Each table must have one or more columns that carry some specific information which uniquely defines an instance of data. This is termed the **primary key**.

In the case of the Customer table, this would likely be the 'Cust. no.' as columns such as 'Name' or 'Address' may not necessarily be unique. The table currently shows two customers living at the same address and it is quite conceivable that there could be two 'Robert Walkers' living in different parts of the country.

CRUCIAL TIP

It is very important to understand the issue of uniqueness during the design stage of a database. Live data entry on a critical system is not the time to find out there are two people with identical names living in the same town!

In the case of the CD table, both 'Song' and 'Artiste' again may not necessarily be unique. This also applies to the columns 'Position', 'Month' and 'Year', for example, in the situation where two copies of the same CD may exist. By numbering each CD with a unique 'CD number' it is a relatively simple task to ensure each record (or row) has a unique value.

Application domain

CRUCIAL CONCEPT

Tables such as 'CD' or 'Customer' are termed **entities**, i.e. things we want to keep data about. Each 'entity' will have several **properties** (columns) and have many 'occurrences' or **instances** (rows). Collectively the various tables would form the **application domain**. In the relational model, all entities must be related to each other to be part of the same **application domain**.

Currently we have a collection of CDs and a collection of customers. As yet we have not specified any relationship between these two tables. The relationship comes into play when CDs are hired out to customers.

CRUCIAL CONCEPT

To enforce a relationship, we simply have to ensure that the 'primary key' of one table exists as a **foreign key** in another. A 'foreign key' is simply the term for an existing primary key that is used in another table as a normal property.

As this is an example of a CD lending library, let us introduce the concept of a hire 'Transaction' linking together a specific record to a specific customer at a specific location on a specific date for a defined duration (see Table 1.3).

Table 1.3 Transaction table

Transaction	CD no.	Cust. no.	Hire date	Duration
00001	0005	004	12/09/02	1
00002	0002	005	13/09/02	2

Table 1.3 shows instances of Queen's CD entitled 'A Kind of Magic' being loaned to Jean Mackie of Sheffield on 12/09/02 for one day as well as the Buck Fizz's CD entitled 'Make Your Mind Up' being loaned to Paul Mackie of Sheffield on 13/09/02 for two days.

Constructing a relational database from form data

Sometimes it is necessary to construct relational databases from forms that may currently be used by the company. If implemented literally, then this may result in data duplication, something that should be avoided with databases as this leads inevitably to data contention, i.e. one piece of data is saying one thing while the same data elsewhere is saying something else.

Consider a typical invoice as the source of data. This may have the following data items:

- invoice number;
- company name;
- address;
- date;
- item quantity;
- item description;
- unit item cost.

If these fields were literally placed in one table and data added, then we would see the result as in Table 1.4.

Table 1.4 Invoice table

Invoice	Company	Address	Date	Qty	Desc.	Cost
0001	IBM	Greenock	13/08/02	1	Computer	1,234.00
0001	IBM	Greenock	13/08/02	1	Printer	324.00
0001	IBM	Greenock	13/08/02	2	Ribbons	13.00
0002	M & S	Sunderland	14/08/02	6	Cameras	234.80
0003	Tesco	Dublin	14/08/02	1	Computer	1,234.00
0003	Tesco	Dublin	14/08/02	3	Printers	324.00

In the case of invoice 0001, the invoice no., the address and date had to be added three times. Similarly for invoice 0003, these properties had to be added twice. What we have is a case of repeating groups.

To solve this type of problem, it is necessary to split the data into different tables. First we create a table collecting all repeating data as in Table 1.5.

Table 1.5 Invoice table

Invoice	Company	Address	Date
0001	IBM	Greenock	13/08/02
0002	M & S	Sunderland	14/08/02
0003	Tesco	Dublin	14/08/02

Then we create another table which we will call 'Item' (see Table 1.6). We have created a primary key called 'Item no.' and included the invoice table primary key as a 'foreign key' thereby establishing a relationship between the two tables

Quick test

1. What are the more common names for relation, attribute and tuple?
2. Give some examples of data that you currently access that is stored in an electronic database.

Table 1.6 Item table

Item no.	Invoice	Qty	Desc.	Cost
00001	0001	1	Computer	1,234.00
00002	0001	1	Printer	324.00
00003	0001	2	Ribbons	13.00
00004	0002	6	Cameras	234.80
00005	0003	1	Computer	1,234.00
00006	0003	1	Printers	324.00

Section 4

Summary

This chapter has given a brief history of the database and the DBMS. It has examined two data models, namely the hierarchical and network models, before going on to discuss the most important development to date, that of the relational model.

In the next chapter we will examine in more depth the relational data model but for now it is important you start to understand the various terminology associated with databases in general and the relational database in particular.

Section 5

End of chapter assessment

Questions

1. a) Describe the impact magnetic disk drives had on database technology.
   b) What was used prior to disk drives?

2. What is the disadvantage of storing data definition within applications?

3. Why is it necessary to understand outdated data models when we have better models available?

4. Explain the concept of primary and foreign keys.

Answers

1. a) Magnetic disk drives allowed data to be accessed at random. Previously all mass storage devices could only store and read data serially. With large databases, sorting would have been virtually impossible. Being able to read data randomly means that data can be sorted or indexed largely at will, allowing data to be viewed in different ways. This is the basis of data modelling.

1. b) Prior to the magnetic disk drive, computers used magnetic tapes, punched cards or even punched paper tapes as their means of mass data storage.

2. Storing data definition within applications can lead to serious data contention issues. Any changes to the data format made in one program would have to be

mirrored in all other programs accessing the same data file. Also a program to read all the existing data and restore this according to the changed format would need to be written.

3. Although there are new and more expressive models now available, we cannot turn our backs on legacy data. If we assume that data is saved for a purpose, then while that purpose still exists, the data cannot be destroyed. There are essentially two options available. Either continue to use the older data models or find a way to migrate the data over to a newer model.

4. A primary key is one or more columns in a relation that either singly or collectively defines an instance of data. It is the portion of data that makes a record unique. A foreign key is simply a primary key from one table used as a simple column or group of columns in another table thus establishing a relationship between the two tables.

Section 6

Further reading

Codd, E. F. (1970) 'A Relational Model of Data for Large Shared Data Banks', *Communications of the ACM*, vol. 13, no. 6, pp. 377–87; reprint available at http://www.acm.org/classics/nov95/.

Connolly, Thomas and Carolyn Begg (2002) *Database Systems*, 3rd edn. Harlow: Addison-Wesley/Pearson Education.

National Research Council (1999) 'The Rise of the Relational Databases', in *Funding a Revolution: Government Support for Computing Research*. Washington, DC: National Academy Press, Chapter 6.

Chapter 2
The relational data model

Chapter summary

Having briefly looked at relational databases using some simple examples, we can now move on to look at the concept of data modelling as applied to the relational model. We will look briefly at the mathematical basis of the model and see how a database can be described and built by examining a series of relations.

Learning outcomes

After studying this chapter, you should check your knowledge against the outcomes below and test your achievement by answering the questions at the end of the chapter. You should be able to:

Outcome 1: Understand the importance of data modelling.
You should be able to describe the ANSI-SPARC three-layer architecture as well as have an appreciation of what constitutes each layer.

Outcome 2: Understand basic set theory.
Basic set theory provides the mathematical framework on which relational database theory is underpinned. You should be able to understand the basis of relations as well as explaining concepts such as primary, foreign and candidate keys.

Outcome 3: Understand relational algebra.
You should be able to understand some of the mathematical concepts as well as carry out many of the manipulations associated with relational algebra.

How will you be assessed on this?

Questions on the purpose of modelling are common in many exams. Depending on the course you are undertaking, you may also be asked to perform some limited exercises in relational algebra. In any event a good understanding of relational algebra will greatly aid later work in the area of Structured Query Language (SQL).

Section 1

Data modelling

Modelling is a technique used in many real-world situations to represent some aspects of a more complex system in order to gain a better understanding of the real system. Consider, for example, a reduced-scale model of a fighter aircraft used in a wind tunnel. Results from a series of tests on such a 'model' can be used directly to influence the shape and contour of the final craft. Of course, models do not have to be purely physical. Consider the modelling carried out by computers in order to reach a predictive weather forecast for presentation on a television channel. It is important to understand that modelling only looks at those aspects of the real-world situation considered important enough to warrant the expense of setting up the model in the first place. Generally, models are a cost-effective means of evaluating a real system, and often the only means of evaluation.

To build a model, we need a basic architecture. At one end is the way users view the data primarily in terms of physical items or according to the processes they use to collect the data. At the other end data relates to how the database will actually use and store the data.

Three-layer architecture

Although the CODASYL database task group (DBTG) initially proposed the use of a two-level model, it was the ANSI-SPARC three-layer model that created most interest (see Figure 2.1). The model comprises:

- an external level;
- a conceptual level;
- an internal Level.

Even although the ANSI-SPARC never became a standard, it is still used as a way to help understanding of how a DBMS functions.

External level: One or more sets of data viewed in terms of real-world issues such as students, lecturers, invoices, statements, etc.

Conceptual level: This is the bridging later between internal and external where some form of mapping has to take place. As we will see, at this level we are more concerned with entities, relationships, constraints, security and integrity.

Internal level: The way data is stored on a physical database. The terminology changes to disk storage, indexes, record description and placement and includes compression and encryption.

Relational modelling is primarily about creating a conceptual model of a process using a set of tables and relationships taken from data in external level or real-world views. It is concerned with the creation of a logical structure of data.

We therefore require a few more definitions to help cement these concepts.

CRUCIAL CONCEPT

An **entity** is a separately identifiable **thing of significance** about which we wish to keep data.

Examples include 'students', 'invoices', 'ships', 'boxers', etc. Relationships between the various entities are a necessary aspect of the database.

CRUCIAL CONCEPT

Attributes are pieces of information about a specific entity.

For example, in the case of an entity called 'student', we might have attributes such as 'age', 'height', 'weight', etc.

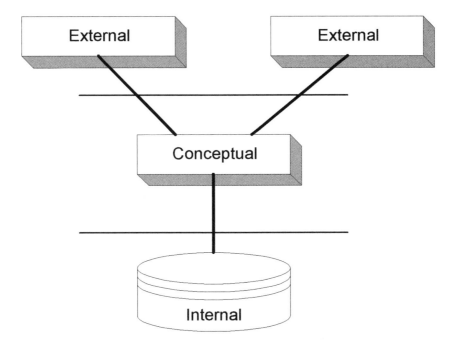

Figure 2.1 ANSI-SPARC three-level architecture

The distinction between an entity and an attribute can often be very confusing. Indeed, there may be no 'correct' solution, much depending on what is demanded from the database. However, within the confines of the model, attributes generally have a direct relationship with only one entity and any reference to that entity applies automatically to its properties.

─────────────── CRUCIAL CONCEPT ───────────────

A **relationship** is the common aspect that links two entities.

For example, banks loan money to customers. If we consider the two entities as being 'Banks' and 'customers', then the relationship would be 'loans'.

Quick test

1. Explain the terms entities, attributes and relationships.
2. Why do we attempt to model data?

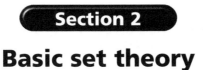
Section 2

Basic set theory

The relational model of data is based on set theory, an area of mathematics developed originally by the Russian mathematician Georg Cantor in 1874. A set is simply a collection of one or more items of the same type. For example a collection of boxers could be {Mohammad Ali, Joe Frazier, Mike Tyson, Lennox Lewis}. A collection of animals could be {A giraffe}. A collection of street numbers could be {No. 11, No. 15, No. 354, No. 74}.

Set theory allows for the concept of a subset simply being part of a set. For example {Mike Tyson, Lennox Lewis} can be considered as a subset of the collection of the earlier boxer set.

Some points of special note are as follows:

- All members of a set must be of the same type – for example, {Mohammad Ali, Joe Frazier, Mike Tyson, Lennox Lewis, a gorilla} is not a valid set.
- The order or sequence of items within a set is not significant.
- Two of the same type cannot exist in the same set. For example: {No. 11, No. 15, No. 11, No. 7} is not permissible as No 11. is a duplicate.

Set theory allows us to take any element from one set along with an element from another set to form what we call an ordered pair. A relation is defined as being a mapping of one element from each set and given a functional name.

Consider two sets as follows:

Set 1={Tiger, Leopard, Zebra, Elephant, Horse}
Set 2={Spots, Squares, Stripes, Triangles}

If we assume a relation based on the skin appearance, then (Tiger, Stripes) could be a valid relation, so also could (Leopard, Spots) and (Zebra, Stripes). Putting this in tabular form yields:

Animal	Skin appearance
Tiger	Stripes
Leopard	Spots
Zebra	Stripes

We can also introduce another set, such as:

Set 3={30, 35, 40, 45, 50}

and map this to the first set based on the top speed of the animal. This could yield a more extensive table of relations such as:

Animal	Skin appearance	Top speed (mph)
Tiger	Stripes	35
Leopard	Spots	45
Zebra	Stripes	40

The total number of relations that can exist between two sets is determined by the Cartesian product, a term we will pick up on in Chapter 12. For now it is important only to note that if we take two sets, for example Set A={3, 5} and Set B={1, 7, 8}, then the Cartesian product of these two sets would be:

A × B={(3, 1), (3, 7), (3, 8), (5, 1), (5, 7), (5, 8)}

Any subset of the Cartesian product is a relation.

It is important to note several things in this regard:

- A relation is represented by a two-dimensional table.
- Each row of the table signifies a separate record.
- No two rows can be identical.
- The order of the rows is not important.
- One or more of the columns represents the primary key of the relation (often called the 'ruling part').
- Columns not forming part of the primary key are often referred to collectively as the 'dependent part'.
- The order of the columns is not important.
- Each column is derived from a set of similar values.
- Columns contain only single values, i.e. no lists.

Important relational concepts

Although set theory provides the mathematical underpinning for relational databases, a full discussion on set theory is outside of the scope of this book. It is essential, however, to appreciate the many relational concepts which apply to the relational database.

Primary key

The concept of a primary key was introduced in Chapter 1 where it was defined as being a column (or columns) which uniquely identify an instance of data. In its simplest form this would be a single column. Consider, for example, a student record system. Although many students study many courses over a period of several years, we can identify a single student by their unique student enrolment number.

Consider the following relation:

Enrol no., Name, Address, Date of birth

By convention the primary key in any set of relations would be underlined. If we now include data, we might end up with the relational table in Table 2.1.

Table 2.1 Student table

Enrol no.	Name	Address	DOB
23786	James Smith	Pan Bank	15/02/79
24564	Hector Jones	Pan Bank	17/08/80
23811	James Smith	The Forge	15/04/78
24345	Angela Jones	Humbleton Hall	17/08/80

It is common within a university or college to have more than one student with the same name, as with this example 'James Smith'. It is also common that several students many live at the same address, for example at a hall of residence. It is also not uncommon that two students share the same birth date, as with 'twins' Hector and Angela Jones. However, no two students would share the same enrolment number. To uniquely identify a student, all we would need is their enrolment number. This is the primary key or 'ruling part'. All other information in the table is dependent on the primary key and called the 'dependent part'.

While many tables have obvious unique keys, there are many instances where a unique key has to be created. Consider for example the CD table used earlier in Chapter 1 (see Table 2.2).

Table 2.2 CD table

CD no.	Song	Artiste	Position	Month	Year
0001	Woman	John Lennon	1	02	1981
0002	Make Your Mind Up	Bucks Fizz	2	04	1981
0003	You Can't Hurry Love	Phil Collins	11	02	1983
0004	It's a Hard Life	Queen	9	07	1984
0005	A Kind of Magic	Queen	5	04	1985
0006	Toy Boy	Sinitta	6	09	1987
0007	You Got It	Roy Orbison	4	02	1989

Here the 'CD no.' has been artificially created at the time of data entry to provide a unique primary key to the table. Most DBMS systems provide some form of automatic number generator for this purpose. The number added has no real significance beyond the fact that it represents the sequence in which the data was added. However, it is guaranteed to be unique.

Composite primary key

In our definition of a primary key, we referred to a column (or columns) which uniquely identify an instance of data. In many cases a single column will not uniquely define an instance of data (a row). If we do not wish to add an extra column containing an auto-generated number, we can combine two or more fields to uniquely create a composite key.

Consider what would happen if we were to use the following Record relation:

Song, Artiste, Position, Month, Year

The result is shown in Table 2.3.

Table 2.3 CD table

Song	Artiste	Position	Month	Year
Woman	John Lennon	1	02	1981
Make Your Mind Up	Bucks Fizz	2	04	1981
You Can't Hurry Love	Phil Collins	11	02	1983
It's a Hard Life	Queen	9	07	1984
A Kind of Magic	Queen	5	04	1985
Toy Boy	Sinitta	6	09	1987
You Got It	Roy Orbison	4	02	1989

Provided the same artiste never reissues the same song title, then the composite key of 'Song, Artiste' could be a valid primary key. 'Song' on its own would soon run into difficulties as many artistes release cover versions of the same music. Others release versions with the same song title that you would swear had no relation at all to the original.

Composite keys are quite common in certain situations, but that will be discussed later.

Functional dependency

It is worth at this stage discussing the concept of **functional dependency**.

Functional dependency is an important concept to grasp. If a column (N) is functionally dependent on another column (M), then every value of M must define uniquely a value of N. This can be written as:

M→N

As an example consider Table 2.4.

Table 2.4 Functional dependency

Supplier	Town/City	County
J. G. Small	Sunderland	Tyne & Wear
Alfred Jones	Poole	Dorset
Flora Green	Sunderland	Tyne & Wear
David Bruce	Buckhaven	Fife
Sarah Cummings	Sunderland	Tyne & Wear
Peter Love	Washington	Tyne & Wear

You will notice in the table that every time 'Sunderland' appears under Town/City, then 'Tyne & Wear' appears in the County field. However every time 'Tyne & Wear' appears in the 'County' field, it does not follow that 'Sunderland' appears in the Town/City field.

Here we can say that County is functionally dependent on Town/City.

Foreign keys

The **foreign key** was introduced earlier as simply the term for an existing primary key that is used in another table as a normal property. It is common to indicate a primary key by either using a dotted underline notation or to include an asterisk after the column name. Consider the example shown in Table 2.5.

Table 2.5(a) Order table

OrderNo	SupplierNo*	Value
1001	101	56.43
1002	102	74.34
1003	102	123.34
1004	101	34.23

Table 2.5(b) Supplier table

SupplierNo	Name	Address	Town
101	John White	Mill Lane	Ryhope
102	Bill Brown	Ocean Road	Pennywell
103	Carole Green	Priestman Way	Boldon

SupplerNo is the primary key in the Supplier table but exists as a foreign key in the Order table. This allows us to relate the information in two tables – for example, OrderNo 1001 has a value of 56.43 and can be linked with the company John White of Mill Lane in Ryhope, both entries sharing the common SupplierNo 101.

It is important to note that this relationship is 'one-way' as depicted by the directed arrowhead. Each foreign key value has only one table entry when used as a primary key. However, each primary key can be used many times as a foreign key. We will explore this further later.

Candidate keys

Sometimes when designing a database, you may come across a situation where two different columns (or combination of columns) could conceivably be used as the primary key. Collectively these would be known as **candidate keys**. Once the primary key has been selected, the other candidate keys would then be called **alternate keys**.

Where there is an obvious primary key, such as SupplierNo or OrderNo, then this would be chosen as the table primary key.

Use of nulls

Another important concept in databases relates to the concept of a **null**.

CRUCIAL CONCEPT

A **null** is essentially no data. It is not the value zero.

Depending on how data arrives, it is possible that not all field information may be available at the time of data entry. In a complex system, for example, database design does not necessarily follow physical form designs. Rather than hold up entry until the missing data is present, we need a simple way of entering what we have and add in the missing information later. We do this by entering a 'null' value.

In reality, a 'null' is simply missing data and is not type checked. It can be used equally well in a text field, a date field, a binary field, etc. At the time of setting up a database table, the designer not only specifies the field type information, but also specifies whether a 'null' is allowed. Clearly there are situations where a 'null' makes no sense, such as a primary key as we would never find the data again.

We will look later at how we can carry out effective queries of a database which has null values present during the SQL tutorial (see Chapter 12).

Quick test

1. Can two rows in a relation be identical?
2. Is the order of the columns important in a relation?

Section 3

Data manipulation using relational algebra

With data represented as a series of relational tables, data manipulation essentially consists of entering, removing, amending and querying the relations.

To accomplish this, relational algebra provides several operators, including:

RESTRICT – also known as SELECT
PROJECT
JOIN
PRODUCT or TIMES
UNION
INTERSECTION
DIFFERENCE

By far the most common of these operators are Restrict, Project and Join.

To best illustrate the operators, let us consider Tables 2.6 and 2.7.

Table 2.6 Requisitions table

Supplier	Date	Town	Transport
JKC	03/10/98	Luton	Rail
Smith	04/10/98	Dundee	Truck
La Coq	04/10/98	Paris	Air

Table 2.7 OrderDetail table

Supplier	PartNo	Qty	Price
JKC	1234	750	35.00
JKC	67A	500	20.74
JKC	67B	1000	10.23
Smith	02342	30	54.34
Smith	AB/1	2000	45.67
La Coq	cd12	10	70.12

RESTRICT

The RESTRICT or SELECT operator takes one relation as an input and outputs a subset of that relation by removing non-matching rows. For example:

RESTRICT OrderDetail WHERE Supplier='Smith'

would return the following relation:

Supplier	PartNo	Qty	Price
Smith	02342	30	54.34
Smith	AB/1	2000	45.67

PROJECT

The PROJECT operator also takes one relation as an input and outputs a subset of that relation by removing non-matching columns. For example:

PROJECT Columns Supplier, Town from Requisitions

would return the following relation:

Supplier	Town
JKC	Luton
Smith	Dundee
La Coq	Paris

JOIN

The JOIN operator differs from the previous two operators in that it takes two relations as its input and produces one relation as its output. For example:

JOIN Tables Requisitions, OrderDetail
      matching Columns Requisitions.Supplier with OrderDetail.Supplier

would return the following relation:

Supplier	Date	Town	Transport	PartNo	Qty	Price
JKC	03/10/98	Luton	Rail	1234	750	35.00
JKC	03/10/98	Luton	Rail	67A	500	20.74
JKC	03/10/98	Luton	Rail	67B	1000	10.23
Smith	04/10/98	Dundee	Truck	02342	30	54.34
Smith	04/10/98	Dundee	Truck	AB/1	2000	45.67
La Coq	04/10/98	Paris	Air	cd12	10	70.12

There are actually three different types of joins, namely:

- NATURAL JOIN, also known as INNER JOIN;
- EQUI-JOIN;
- OUTER JOIN.

We have in fact illustrated the NATURAL or INNER JOIN where the output only contains one copy of the matching columns. With the EQUI-JOIN, both matching columns would remain in the output relation.

The OUTER JOIN tends to be more complex having to deal with three separate ways of joining two tables and is not covered in this Study Text.

PRODUCT

The PRODUCT is similar to a JOIN in that it takes two relations as its input and produces one output, this time composed of every possible combination of the input rows. In set theory it is known as the Cartesian product. It has limited practical value because of its ability to create a 'data explosion', i.e. the resulting output relation being so large as to be practically useless.

UNION, INTERSECTION and DIFFERENCE

For the UNION, INTERSECTION and DIFFERENCE operators these can only be applied to tables which have the same structure. Consider the situation where two companies maintain a database detailing where they source critical supplies (see Tables 2.8 and 2.9).

Table 2.8 CompanyA

Supplier	Town	Transport
Bells	Bristol	Rail
Smith	Dundee	Truck
La Coq	Paris	Air

Table 2.9 CompanyB

Supplier	Town	Transport
JKC	Luton	Rail
Jones	Cardiff	Rail
Smith	Dundee	Truck
Martins	Glassow	Air

In this example, both CompanyA and CompanyB use the services of Smith from Dundee.

UNION

A UNION combines the rows from both tables, removing any redundant rows in the process. Hence the statement:

CompanyA UNION CompanyB

would produce:

Supplier	Town	Transport
Bells	Bristol	Rail
Smith	Dundee	Truck
La Coq	Paris	Air
JKC	Luton	Rail
Jones	Cardiff	Rail
Martins	Glasgow	Air

DIFFERENCE

The DIFFERENCE operator subtracts any common rows that appear in both tables from a particular table. Thus A − B subtracts the common rows from A and B − A would subtract the common rows from B.

As an example, CompanyA DIFFERENCE CompanyB would yield:

Supplier	Town	Transport
Bells	Bristol	Rail
La Coq	Paris	Air

INTERSECTION

The INTERSECTION of two tables or relations in a similar way outputs only the common rows that exist in both tables. Thus:

CompanyA INTERSECTION CompanyB

would yield:

Supplier	Town	Transport
Smith	Dundee	Truck

Relational operators

The above relational operators provide much of the basis for a database query language such as SQL. We will explore this in more detail in later chapters.

Relational views

Relational databases provide another very powerful feature called **relational views**. A view is the result produced by a relational query and held as a virtual table. This permits the DBMS to access this output relation as though it were in fact a real database table. This can greatly speed up certain types of applications, for example by running a query once and processing, say, a set of reports out of the resulting relation. It is also useful for allowing different users to view the same data in wholly different ways.

Quick test

1. What are the three most common relational algebra operators?
2. Describe what each of these three operators is used for.

Summary

The ANSI-SPARC architecture provides a convenient way of mapping real-world problems into a relational database solution. We have also looked closely at much of the mathematical underpinning of the relational model which we are going to use in the succeeding chapters. Armed with this knowledge, we are about ready to start the journey from real-world problem to an effective integrated database solution utilising relational database techniques.

End of chapter assessment

Questions

1. Explain the three layers of the ANSI-SPARC architecture.

2. Explain the difference between a primary key and a candidate key as applied to a relational database.

3. Using Tables 2.10 and 2.11, work out the following relational algebra operations:
   a) Difference of Company 1 – Company 2;
   b) Difference of Company 2 – Company 1;

c) Union of Company 1 and Company 2;
d) Intersection of Company 1 and Company 2.

Table 2.10 Company 1

ProductNo	Supplier	Location
B0002	Gregson	Glasgow
B0004	Smith	Linlithgow
B0005	Davis	Cardiff
B0006	Powell	New York
B0009	Marshall	Dublin

Table 2.11 Company 2

ProductNo	Supplier	Location
B0009	Marshall	Dublin
B0007	Steele	Belfast
B0005	Davis	Cardiff

Answers

1. The three layers of the ANSI-SPARC architecture are:
   a) External layer;
   b) Conceptual layer;
   c) Internal layer.

   The external layer essentially deals with real-world issues such as companies, students, people, salaries, etc.

   The conceptual layer deals with entities, relationships, constraints, security and integrity.

   The internal layer deals with disk storage, records, compression and encryption.

   The three layers provide a mapping between the human view (at the external level), the information systems view (at the conceptual layer) through to the physical disk storage (at the internal level).

2. Candidate keys are columns or combinations of columns that can be used to uniquely define a record (row) in a relational database. There can often be several candidate keys available. One of the candidate keys becomes the primary key and information to this effect is passed to the DBMS for subsequent processing. The remaining candidate keys are then termed alternate keys.

3. a) The difference of Company 1 – Company 2 is essentially the records for Company 1 minus any common records that also appear in Company 2, i.e.

ProductNo	Supplier	Location
B0002	Gregson	Glasgow
B0004	Smith	Linlithgow
B0006	Powell	New York

   b) The difference of Company 2 – Company 1 is essentially the records of Company 2 minus any common records that also appear in Company 1, i.e.

ProductNo	Supplier	Location
B0007	Steele	Belfast

c) The Union of Company 1 and Company 2 is an amalgamation of all records without duplication, i.e.

ProductNo	Supplier	Location
B0002	Gregson	Glasgow
B0004	Smith	Linlithgow
B0005	Davis	Cardiff
B0006	Powell	New York
B0009	Marshall	Dublin
B0007	Steele	Belfast

d) The Intersection of Company 1 and Company 2 is the records common to Company 1 and Company 2, i.e.

ProductNo	Supplier	Location
B0005	Davis	Cardiff
B0009	Marshall	Dublin

Section 6

Further reading

Green, J. A. (1988) *Sets and Groups: A First Course in Algebra*. London and New York: Routledge & Kegan Paul.

Chapter 3
The entity-relational model

Chapter summary

As we saw in the last chapter, relational modelling looks mainly at the conceptual layer of the three level ANSI-SPARC architecture. Entity-relational modelling, on the other hand, is more concerned with the modelling of items within the real-world domain. In particular it looks at the various types of relationships that can exist between different entities. Often referred to simply as ER modelling, it takes a diagrammatic look at how the various entities of a database fit together. In this chapter we will introduce some new terms such as cardinality (sometimes called the degree of a relationship) as well as optionality.

While much of the work associated with relational modelling is directly attributed to Ted Codd in 1970, entity-relational modelling is associated closely with Peter Chen following the release of a paper entitled 'The Entity-Relational Model – Towards a Unified View of Data' (Chen, 1976).

Learning outcomes

After studying this chapter, you should check your knowledge against the outcomes below and test your achievement by answering the questions at the end of the chapter. You should be able to:

Outcome 1: Understand the difference between entities and entity types.
You should be able to explain the difference between entities and entity types, one of the key elements of ER modelling.

Outcome 2: Understand the various types of relationships.
While one-to-one and one-to-many relationships can be handled within a relational database, many-to-many relationships cannot. You should be able to resolve many-to-many relationships into their lesser counterparts. You should also understand some of the more unusual forms of relationships that can arise.

Outcome 3: Understand the meaning of optionality and how it is applied.
You should be able to recognise and apply optionality to the various relationships.

Outcome 4: Understand how attributes link into entity types.
You should be able to discuss the meaning of attributes and their association to entity types.

How will you be assessed on this?

Assessment will come in two forms. The first part will likely be a short series of questions to test your understanding of key concepts. The second part will likely be a short piece of text describing a potential system. You will be asked to draw a typical ER diagram for the system clearly identifying the key parts such as entities, entity types, attributes and relationships, also indicating cardinality and optionality.

Section 1

Entities and entity types

We defined an entity earlier as a separately identifiable 'thing of significance' about which we want to keep data. Attempting to identify entities needs some thought and an understanding of the real-world problem. Often the starting point for any database design will be a piece of written text produced by someone who will understand the problem but who may not have any knowledge of databases. Consider, for example the following text:

> Each academic area within the university is part of a single school. Each school has a number of academic areas, depending on the size of the school. For example, Software Engineering Academic Area has as one of its staff members James Knight who is part of the School of Computing. Internet Technologies is another academic area which is also part of the School of Computing.

Clearly not everything is being said here although the statement of the problem domain is fairly clear. We might be able to deduce, for example, that there are several schools within the university each of which has a unique name. What we should also be able to deduce are the 'things of significance' we will likely want to keep data on and which have relationships with other 'things of significance', namely Schools, Academic areas and Staff members.

CRUCIAL TIP

It should be noted here that a relationship must involve two or more entity types. If only one entity type is involved, then this should not be considered a relationship but merely a property or attribute of that entity type.

While schools such as the School of Computing can be an entity, we can define a 'school' as an **entity type**. In other words, an entity type is defined as a group of entities that can be said to have a common definition. Similarly 'Academic area' is an entity type of which Internet Technologies is an example entity.

The important thing to understand about entity types is that these are concepts rather than physical instances. Consider an entity type called City. This is indeed a concept which in turn can have instances such as London, Edinburgh, Sunderland and Newcastle. Entity types are singular (referring to the concept) although there may be many City entities.

Looking back at the given text, we can now spot the entities and entity types (see Table 3.1).

Table 3.1 Entities and entity types

Entity type	Entities
School	School of Computing
Academic area	Software Engineering
	Internet Technologies
Staff member	James Knight

Clearly there will be a great deal more entities but no doubt these will be revealed later in the design exercise. What we are more concerned about at this stage are the entity types.

We are also able to start identifying relationships between entity types. In the original paper, Peter Chen represented relationships using diamonds and entity types using rectangles. Therefore the following would graphically represent the above scenario:

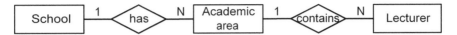

Although this style is still used, there are many other notations that have been adopted by analysts such as UML (see Section 5) and crow's feet. We will adopt the crow's feet notation for the purposes of this book as it is one of the most popular and tends to reinforce concepts more graphically than Chen's original notation.

We can represent the above diagram in crow's foot notation as:

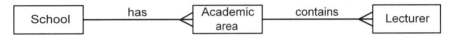

Notice the crow's feet in the relationships showing here that there are several instances of type academic area in a school and that there are several instances of type lecturer in an academic area. We will develop this notation as we work through the many possibilities of modelling data using this technique.

Quick test

What do we mean by an entity type?

Section 2

Types of relationships

Essentially the vast majority of relationships between entity types fall in one of three main categories as listed in Table 3.2.

Table 3.2 Categories of entity types

Description	Symbolic	Example
One to One	1 : 1	A managing director manages a company
One to Many	1 : n	A company employs many engineers
Many to Many	m : n	Many engineers work on many projects

─── CRUCIAL CONCEPT ───

Cardinality is the specific name given to the number of entities of one type that can be associated with the number of entities of another type. This is also termed the **degree of the relationship**.

Consider the typical company shown in Figure 3.1.

A managing director manages a company. We have assumed here that he only manages one company and that he does not share this post with any other. This is

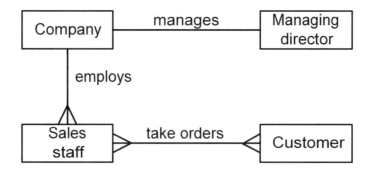

Figure 3.1 A typical company

therefore shown as a 1:1 relationship. We can also make the association in two directions, namely:

- One managing director manages one company.
- One company is managed by one managing director.

In the case of the relationship between Company and Sales staff, this is a 1:Many relationship (sometimes called a 1:n relationship). Again we can make the association in two directions, namely:

- One company employs one or more Sales staff.
- One Sales staff is employed by one company.

Notice the crow's foot on the 'many' side of the relationship.

In the relationship between Customer and Sales staff, we can see the Many-to-Many relationship (sometimes called the m:n relationship). Here we make the association as:

- Each customer places their orders with one or more Sales staff.
- Each member of the Sales staff takes orders from one or more Customers.

Notice the use of the crow's foot at both ends of the relationship.

Many-to-many relationships are common and of use during the early part of an ER diagram. Consider what happens in the above situation, however, if you wanted to trace through a customer's order. Unfortunately there is no direct mapping between a specific order and a specific member of the Sales staff. What is needed is a further step to make the necessary association.

To resolve this issue we need to introduce a linking entity with whom both original entities can be said to have a relationship. For instance, in the above example, we could introduce the concept of an 'order' entity to change the original relationship:

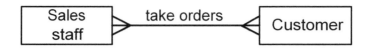

into a new relationship:

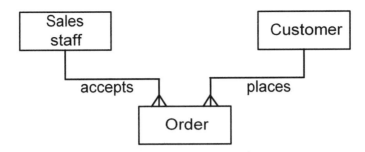

Here the entity 'Order' can be said to uniquely define an instance involving both 'Sales staff' and 'Customer'. Now, instead of having a single 'many-to-many' relationship, we have created two 'one-to-many' relationships which and be evaluated successfully by a database.

Quick test

Describe the three main types of entity relationships

Section 3

Optionality

Optionality is the specific name given to a relationship which may or may not exist.

In the company example above, we may want to look more closely at the Company to Sales staff relationship.

- One company employs one or more Sales staff.
- One Sales staff is employed by one company.

What would happen if one of the Sales staff did not work for a company but was part of a special product promotion by an outside agency? We would have to modify the second part of the relationship to read:

- One Sales staff is employed by the company or no company.

Diagrammatically this could be represented by a circle at one end and a bar (or '1') at the other. These signify the minimum and maximum occurrences that can exist, i.e. (zero or one) at the company end and (one or more than one) at the Sales staff end:

An alternative way of representing optionality is through the use dotted and full lines. The dotted line signifies a 'may' relationship and a full line signifies a 'must' relationship. This is illustrated in the following example:

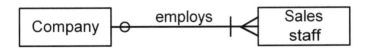

i.e.

- One company must employ one or more Sales staff.
- One Sales staff may be employed by the company.

Quick test

Explain what we mean by optionality.

Section 4

Attributes

So far we have concentrated our discussions on entity types and relationships. Now we need to look at the remaining information that we are interested in collecting, namely that which we generally refer to as either attributes or properties. An attribute is an item whose value is associated with a specific entity type.

Attributes are items of data which can only take up one value at any particular point in time. This may vary over time, such as a person's address or salary, but would be fixed for a specific time yielding only one value if queried by different users in the same time frame.

Diagrammatically, attributes are introduced into an ER diagram in a variety of ways. One popular method is through the introduction of ellipses, each ellipse representing an attribute (see Figure 3.2). The problem with this approach is that a diagram soon gets too complicated and defeats the point of using it.

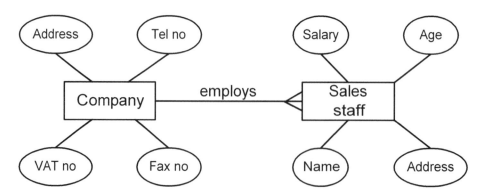

Figure 3.2 One method of depiction of attributes in an ER diagram

An alternative style and one favoured by most computer-aided software engineering (CASE) tools is shown in Figure 3.3.

The work of a data analyst in designing a new relational database system is to try and understand fully the real-world problem in order to be able to describe the information (largely diagrammatically) in terms of entities, relationships and attributes.

Quick test

Explain the difference between an attribute and an entity type.

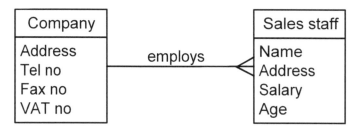

Figure 3.3 Preferred method of depiction of attributes in an ER diagram

Section 5

Other types of relationships

Most relationships involve the relationship between two entities and hence are called binary relationships. However, there are other types of relationships that can exist in ER modelling.

Unary or recursive relationship

A **unary** relationship is one in which a relation exists between members of the same entity type. For example:

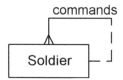

Note the use of optionality here where we can say that a soldier may command more than one soldier.

Ternary relationship

A **ternary** relationship is more complex involving three entities as part of only one relationship. Take the situation where college students must attend lectures at a specific college campus:

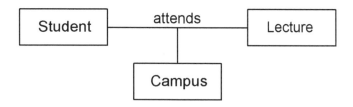

It is difficult to express cardinality on this type of relationship as this would likely be ambiguous with respect to the other entities.

To resolve this type of situation it is necessary to change this relationship into something we can reasonably deal with such as:

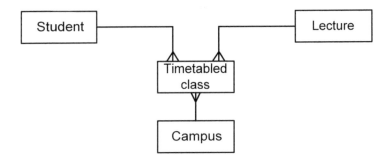

Here we have brought in the concept of a 'Timetabled class' entity which has 'one-to-many' relationships with the original three entities as shown above.

Multiple relationships

Of course we are not limited to only one relationship existing between two entities at the same time. Take, for instance, the relationship between a 'Person' and a 'Car'. In one situation this may simply be to describe the relationship of ownership. In another this may be to describe the activity of driving, thus:

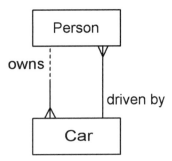

Here the relationships show that a person may or may not own one or more cars. It also shows that a car can be driven by one or more persons.

Exclusive relationship

Sometimes there can be different relationships that can exist between different entities that are in fact mutually exclusive. Take the situation where a company makes either a cash sale or an account sale. In the first case customers will be issued with a sales receipt. In the second case the customers will be issued with an invoice. During the evaluation it may be a simple matter of having two entity types – one called Cash customer and another called Account customer. Alternatively it may be easier to show exclusivity in the relationship, thus:

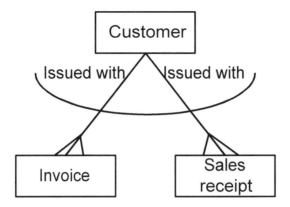

Other modelling forms

While entity-relationship modelling is still the most common modelling technique for relational databases, it should be said that a growing band of followers are starting to use the Unified Modelling Language (UML). UML made an immediate impact in object-oriented designs but is also being used to model object-relational as well as relational systems.

Quick test

Give another example of a ternary relationship from that listed in this chapter.

Summary

In this chapter we have looked at one of the major techniques for analysing real-world database problems, namely the entity-relational (ER) diagram. ER diagrams take textual information and put it into a form that can be readily converted later to tables and relationships in preparation for incorporation into a relational database. Of special interest within these diagrams will be the various many-to-many relationships which will need to be resolved before we can proceed.

End of chapter assessment

Questions

1. Define the following terms:
    a) entity;
    b) entity type;
    c) optionality;
    d) the degree of a relationship.

2. Draw an ER diagram for the following system clearly identifying any assumptions you have made in your solution. The ER diagram must include all known attributes and entities as well as defining cardinality and optionality of the various relationships.

Note that any many-to-many relationships must be resolved and define likely primary keys within the attributes.

An electronics development company wishes to keep information on all the products it develops. Each project carries its own product number as well as a description and expected completion date. Each project will be subdivided into a group of development tasks with each task having a description and an associated budget. Although each task will carry an identifier, this will only be unique within the context of the project and not across the various projects. An engineer will be assigned either one or a group of tasks to carry out, although some of these tasks will have more than one engineer assigned to it. Tasks have to be defined for each project although these do not necessarily have to be defined at the start of the project. The system to be developed should record both the employee number and name

Answers

1. a) Entity is essentially something that you wish to keep data on. It can be an employee, an invoice, a vehicle, etc.
   b) An entity type is a more generalised description of specific entities that you plan to keep data on. For example, Mr Green, Mr Brown, Mr Blue and Mr Pink might be staff you plan to keep data on. The entity type would likely be something like Employee with Mr Green being an instance of an employee. In other words, an entity type is a group of entities that can be said to have a common definition and type.
   c) Optionality is the 'strength' of the relationship, i.e. whether it is mandatory or optional.
   d) The degree of a relationship is its cardinality, i.e. whether it is one-to-one, one-to-many or indeed many-to-many.

2. From the text there are three identifiable entities, namely Engineers, Projects and Tasks. However, it is also clear that the relationship between Engineers and Tasks is a many-to-many relationship requiring to be broken down using a made-up entity. We have called this link entity an 'Assignment'.

This yields the ER diagram shown in Figure 3.4.

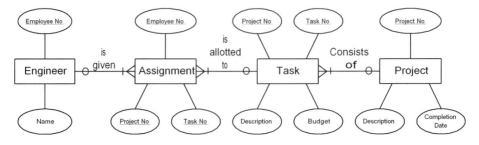

Figure 3.4 ER diagram

Section 8

Further reading

Blaha, Michael and William Premerlani (1998) *Implementing UML Models with Relational Databases*, available at http://www.therationaledge.com/rosearchitect/mag/archives/9904/RATL-2.PDF, accessed December 2002.

Chen, Peter P. (1976) 'The Entity-Relational Model – Towards a Unified View of Data', *ACM Transactions on Database Systems*, vol. 1, no. 1, March 1976; also available from Dr Peter Chen's Website at the Louisiana State University, http://bit.csc.lsu.edu/~chen/, accessed November 2002.

Lejk, Mark and David Deeks (2002) *An Introduction to Systems Analysis Techniques*, 2nd edn. London: Addison Wesley Press.

OMG (2003) *OMG Unified Modeling Language Specification Version 1.5 March 2003*, available at http://www.omg.org/technology/documents/formal/uml.htm, accessed March 2003.

Chapter 4
Constructing relational tables from ER diagrams

Chapter summary

In this chapter we are going to look at some typical ER diagram relationships (along with details of the various entity properties) and produce a set of relational tables. At this stage these tables will not be optimised – this is something we will look at closer in the next chapter. For the present we want to discuss the basic process in going from a graphical ER modelling diagram to a set of relational tables.

Learning outcomes

After studying this chapter, you should check your knowledge against the outcomes below and test your achievement by answering the questions at the end of the chapter. You should be able to:

Outcome 1: Transpose an ER diagram to a set of relational tables.
You should be able to identify relationships as well as data that simply appear as properties.

Outcome 2: Resolve any remaining many-to-many relationships.
You should be able resolve any remaining complex relationships into simple one-to-one or one-to-many relationships.

How will you be assessed on this?

You will likely be given a simple ER diagram and be requested to transpose the data into a set of relational tables. You will need to be clear on aspects such as primary keys and foreign keys, particularly with regard to aspects such as referential integrity.

Section 1

Getting started

The process involved in transposing an ER diagram into a set of relational tables can be either very complex or relatively straightforward. If the system analysis has been performed well, generally this is a straightforward process. At this stage we should not be overly concerned about whether the tables are structured in the most efficient manner – that step comes later. We will be introducing you to the process of normalisation which is a set of routines to follow to ensure that the tables do not contain any redundancy. For now we are more concerned with transposing the real-world requirements of the ER diagrams into relational tables.

The process generally involves three basic steps:

- Create entity tables using all attributes as well as cardinality found on the ER diagram.
- Where any many-to-many relationships still exist on the ER diagram, these must be resolved using additional entity types (link entities).
- Indicate both primary and foreign keys in the form of linkages between the tables.

Creating tables

In order to correctly transpose ER diagrams into sets of relational tables, we need to consider two parts. The first is purely that associated with table creation. The second takes on board the many issues of cardinality and optionality.

Let's consider a relationship between a lecturer and a course with no cardinality indicated, thus:

We can start by preparing a table for each entity type where each column represents an attribute and each instance of the entity is represented by a separate row. Primary keys must be unique to ensure that no two rows can refer to the same set of data. In many cases these keys will be obvious but in situations where it is not obvious it may be necessary to use automatic number generators (a special data type used by the DBMS) to produce a series of unique sequential numbers for every row of data entered. Generally these attributes would be called suitable names such as LecturerID or LecturerNo.

Example data for the two entities is given in Tables 4.1 and 4.2.

Table 4.1 Lecturer

LecturerID	Name
123	J. K. Smith
201	R. L. Warrender
305	P. R. Todd

Table 4.2 Course

CourseID	Title	Credits
COM166	Computer Systems	10
COM264	IT Environments	20
COP203	Networks for Business	20

Quick test

Outline the basic steps involved in transposing the real-world requirements of the ER diagrams into relational tables.

Consideration of cardinality

Now let us take on board the various issues concerning cardinality.

One-to-one relationship

Where we have a 'one-to-one' relationship we have the option of using one or two tables. If we combine into one table then we have the possibility of using either of the two primary keys provided the relationship exists in both directions (mandatory). If, however, the relationship is optional in one direction (for example when a course exists but is currently not taught) then the primary key must be that of the mandatory relationship. If both relationships are optional then the data must be left in two tables.

For the present we will assume that all lecturers do teach on one course and that all courses are taught by one lecturer. In Table 4.3 we have used LecturerID as the primary key.

Table 4.3 Lecturer

LecturerID	Name	CourseID	Title	Credits
123	J. K. Smith	COP203	Networks for Business	20
201	R. L. Warrender	COM166	Computer Systems	10
305	P. R. Todd	COM264	IT Environments	20

The more flexible approach, however, would be to keep the two tables separate. To relate the two tables we simply have to make the primary key of one table a 'foreign key' of the other. This would yield one of two solutions, either Table 4.4 or 4.5.

Table 4.4(a) Lecturer

LecturerID	Name	CourseID
123	J. K. Smith	COP203
201	R. L. Warrender	COM166
305	P. R. Todd	COM264

Table 4.4(b) Course

CourseID	Title	Credits
COM166	Computer Systems	10
COM264	IT Environments	20
COP203	Networks for Business	20

Table 4.5(a) Lecturer

LecturerID	Name
123	J. K. Smith
201	R. L. Warrender
305	P. R. Todd

Table 4.5(b) Course

CourseID	Title	Credits	LecturerID
COM166	Computer Systems	10	201
COM264	IT Environments	20	305
COP203	Networks for Business	20	123

Note also the common practice of underlining the 'foreign key' with a dotted line.

One-to-many relationship

Where we have a 'one-to-many' relationship we have the option of using either two or three tables.

Assume we have the following relationship:

The assumption here is that one lecturer teaches one or more courses but that a single course is taught by one lecturer.

Using the two-tabled approach relies on the fact here that each course is delivered by a single lecturer, therefore we can safely take the primary key of the Lecturer table (Table 4.6(a)) for inclusion into the Course table (Table 4.6(b)).

Table 4.6(a) Lecturer

LecturerID	Name
123	J. K. Smith
201	R. L. Warrender
305	P. R. Todd

Table 4.6(b) Course

CourseID	Title	Credits	LecturerID
COM166	Computer Systems	10	201
COM182	Visual Basic	20	123
COM186	Systems Analysis	20	305
COM224	Nets & Comms	10	201
COM264	IT Environments	20	305
COP203	Networks for Business	20	123

Many-to-many relationship

In a 'many-to-many' relationship, we have no option but to use a three-table approach. Note that in some circles leaving a 'many-to-many' relationship on an ER diagram would be considered incomplete and should have been resolved into three entities prior to completion.

Here we are saying that a lecturer can teach more than one course and that a course can be taught by more than one lecturer. Again the third table would be an association table consisting of the primary keys from both tables and given a suitable name.

Thus to resolve this type of problem we have first to resolve the many-to-many relationship, if not on paper then certainly in our minds. Many-to-many relationships as they stand cannot map directly to relational tables.

An example of this is shown in Table 4.7.

Table 4.7(a) Lecturer

LecturerID	Name
123	J. K. Smith
201	R. L. Warrender
305	P. R. Todd

Table 4.7(b) Course

CourseID	Title	Credits
COM166	Computer Systems	10
COM182	Visual Basic	20
COM186	Systems Analysis	20
COM224	Nets & Comms	10
COM264	IT Environments	20
COP203	Networks for Business	20

Table 4.7(c) Course staff

CourseID	LecturerID
COM166	123
COM166	201
COM182	123
COM182	305
COM186	305
COM224	201
COM264	305
COP203	123

Quick test

Describe how you would transpose a many-to-many relationship into set of relational tables. How many tables would be involved?

Section 3

Summary

We have not necessarily reached the optimum solution but we have considered the various options that can arise within an ER diagram and mapped these onto relational tables. How well we have done will become more clear as we progress through the optimisation (normalisation) phase. In theory, though, if we have correctly interpreted the real-world requirements in the form of an ER diagram and followed the rules on transposing this over to relational tables, we will have a system that can be built.

End of chapter assessment

Question

Consider the ER diagram shown in Figure 4.1. Transform the diagram into a relational schema that shows referential integrity constraints.

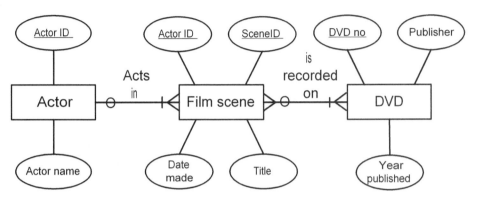

Figure 4.1 ER diagram

Answer

Between Actor and Film scene, there is a one-to-many relationship. To resolve this we will use a simple two-table approach.

We can start with Actor, which can be transposed to a table, thus:

Actor

ActorID	Actor Name

'ActorID' would be the primary key with a single attribute called 'Actor name'.

The second table would be the Film scene entity – also straightforward in terms of fields, namely:

Film scene

ActorID	SceneID	Date made	Scene title

In the case of the cardinality between DVD and Film scene, we have a many-to-many relationship requiring a three-table approach. To resolve the many-to-many relationship we will use a linking entity (in this case Film). A film consists of many film scenes and a film can be stored on one or more DVDs.

As with most linking entities, we can use the primary key of one entity **plus** the primary key of the second entity to be the primary key for the linking entity. Thus we get first for the DVD:

DVD

DVD no.	Publisher	Year published

and for the film:

FILM

ActorID	SceneID	DVD no.	Title

Notice that Title belongs to the Film and not the DVD as there could be more than one DVD per film.

We can then collect these together in one composite diagram (Figure 4.2) showing both the primary and foreign key relationships.

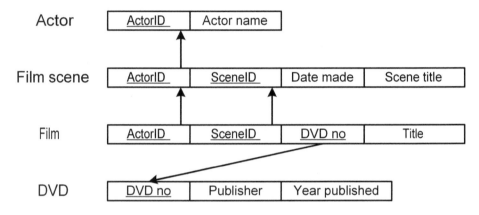

Figure 4.2 Primary and foreign relationships

Chapter 5
Database normalisation

Chapter summary

When moving data from the real world to relational databases, we often face difficulties trying to ensure that data is only held once within the system and that the same data does not reappear in another table. Apart from being wasteful of space, a far more compelling reason is to ensure that any change made to a specific item (say a telephone number) is automatically used by every part of the database system. If two copies of the same telephone number existed then discrepancies could easily arise should only one of these numbers be changed. This chapter looks in detail at the process of normalisation, in particular the first, second and third normal forms.

Learning outcomes

After studying this chapter, you should check your knowledge against the outcomes below and test your achievement by answering the questions at the end of the chapter. You should be able to:

Outcome 1: Understand the reason for normalisation.
You should be able to describe the phases of normalisation and what must be done at each step.

Outcome 2: Carry out normalisation to third normal form.
Starting with a set of un-normalised data available in relational table format, you should be able to go through the steps of normalisation (1NF, 2NF and 3NF).

How will you be assessed on this?

Normalisation is always popular for exams. You will likely be asked to define the first three stages of normalisation (1NF, 2NF and 3NF), setting out clearly what you must do to achieve the various stages. After that you will likely be given a sample problem with a description or a relationship with its known dependencies. Either way you will be asked to normalise the data to 3NF clearly showing your intermediate steps.

Section 1

Introduction to normalisation

Normalisation is a fairly methodical process exercising a set of definable rules in order to arrive at a robust table arrangement. As we will see, the process relies heavily on knowledge of the data. There are several levels of normalisation which we will group as follows:

1NF	–	First normal form
2NF	–	Second normal form
3NF	–	Third normal form
BCNF	–	Boyce-Codd normal form
4NF	–	Fourth normal form
5NF	–	Fifth normal form
DK/NF	–	Domain-key normal form

In terms of importance, 1NF, 2NF and 3NF are by far the most important and should be considered as mandatory for all practical relational databases. BCNF is a more rigorous form of 3NF and should be applied to production databases. 4NF, 5NF and DK/NF are not generally considered as these deal with situations considered to be very rare.

Initially only three forms of normalisation (1NF, 2NF and 3NF) were put forward by E. F. Codd in 1972. The Boyce-Codd normal form was later introduced by R. Boyce and E. F. Codd in 1974. The later forms were mainly the work of R. Fagin in the period from 1977 through to 1981.

Going beyond third normal form is outside the scope of this book. Before we go into detail on the process of normalisation, we will first summarise the steps to be taken to achieve third normal form. These are shown in Figure 5.1.

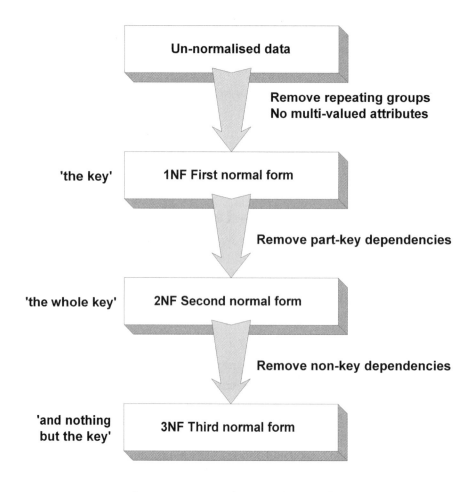

Figure 5.1 Steps to achieve third normal form

Case study

Let's consider an example where we may want to commit to a database the details of packing notes raised by a supplier. The fields involved on the packing note might be as shown in Figure 5.2.

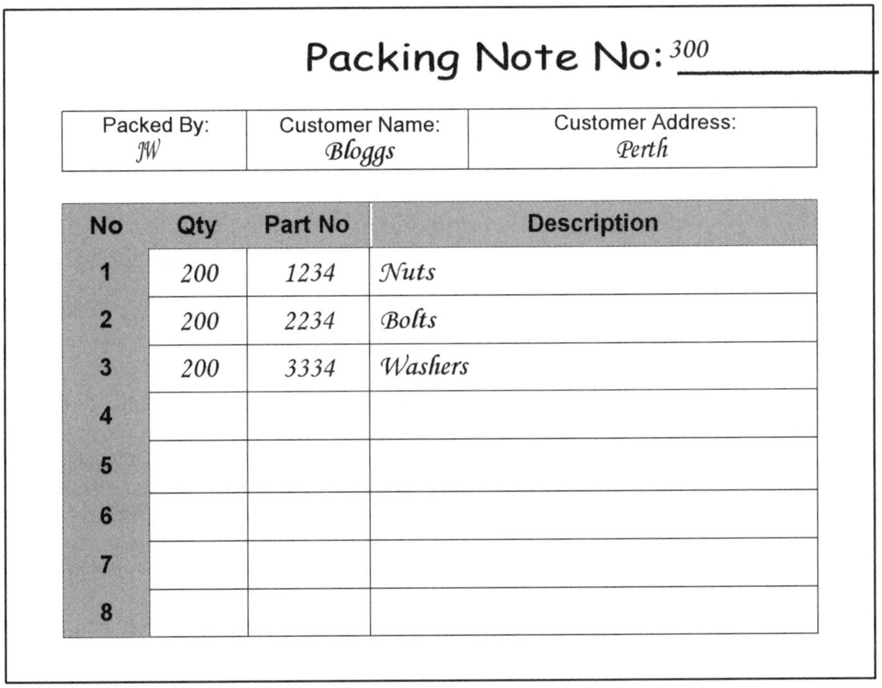

Packing Note No: *300*

Packed By: *JW*	Customer Name: *Bloggs*	Customer Address: *Perth*

No	Qty	Part No	Description
1	*200*	*1234*	*Nuts*
2	*200*	*2234*	*Bolts*
3	*200*	*3334*	*Washers*
4			
5			
6			
7			
8			

Figure 5.2 Packing note

Un-normalised data

The first important fact to realise is that there are fields which appear only once on the packing note (those in the header group) and there are fields that repeat for every separate item listed on the packing note (those in the invoice body group). If we were to try to make one record for each packing note, this would result as shown in Table 5.1:

Table 5.1 Un-normalised data

NoteNo	Packer	Name	Address	ItemNo	Qty	PartNo	Desc
300	JW	Bloggs	Perth	1	200	1234	Nuts
				2	200	2234	Bolts
				3	200	3334	Washers

Here we can clearly identify repeating groups. But fields must be 'atomic' in the sense that there can only be one value in any field (no multi-valued attributes).

In theory we could extend the number of columns and introduce the following fields:

Item 1 Quantity
Item 1 Part Number
Item 1 Description
Item 2 Quantity
Item 2 Part Number
Item 2 Description
Item 3 Quantity
Item 3 Part Number
Item 3 Description
etc.

However, this has many problems associated with it. First, we do not know in advance the number of separate items on any particular packing note. This would result in having to cater for the maximum possible number of items that could be expected. The vast majority of entries would likely be much less than this maximum making the database unnecessarily large. It would also make queries much less efficient as we would have to search for the required data in multiple columns.

1NF – first normal form

A better approach would be to repeat the common data to ensure that this resulted in storage only of atomic values, as in Table 5.2.

Table 5.2 First normal form

NoteNo	Packer	CoName	CoAddress	ItemNo	Qty	PartNo	Desc
300	JW	Bloggs	Perth	1	200	1234	Nuts
300	JW	Bloggs	Perth	2	200	2234	Bolts
300	JW	Bloggs	Perth	3	200	3334	Washers

Although satisfying the issue of atomic values, clearly a great deal of redundancy has been introduced. Nevertheless this table satisfies the rules of 1NF.

An alternative approach at this stage would be to split the table into two parts. Not surprisingly, going either route should end up with much the same solution although arguably the second approach is perhaps a quicker way of getting to 2NF. For the moment we will proceed with the single table.

2NF – second normal form

To be in 2NF we must remove any part-key dependencies. (For a discussion on functional dependency see Chapter 2, section 2.)

Here we quickly run into a problem. NoteNo cannot by itself be used as a key as this is not unique. We must therefore consider the use of a composite key (i.e. one containing more than one column). By looking at the table data, it should be apparent that a key would have to utilise both the NoteNo as well as ItemNo. A different NoteNo would be used for a different despatch but is not unique for every line. An ItemNo would be unique within the context of a single packing note but not necessarily between different despatch notes – conceivably you may ship the same item to two different customers.

Let's have a look at the implications of using a composite key consisting of NoteNo and ItemNo. This would work as a primary key but would fail on the dependency issue as we have part-key dependencies. The reason for this is that fields such as Packer, CoName and CoAddress are dependent only on NoteNo whereas fields Qty, PartNo and Desc would be dependent on the composite key NoteNo and ItemNo. To solve this problem we have to split the table (as we suggested when we looked at 1NF) as Tables 5.3 and 5.4.

Table 5.3 PackingNote

NoteNo	Packer	CoName	CoAddress
300	JW	Bloggs	Perth

Table 5.4 PackingNoteItem

NoteNo	ItemNo	Qty	PartNo	Desc
300	1	200	1234	Nuts
300	2	200	2234	Bolts
300	3	200	3334	Washers

We can consider 2NF to consist of two tables:

- PackingNote (NoteNo, Packer, CoName, CoAddress);
- PackingNoteItem (NoteNo, ItemNo, Qty, PartNo, Desc).

It is interesting to note that this is the same solution we would have achieved for 1NF (as well as 2NF) had we simply split tables from the outset. Although splitting tables at the start does not always make the transition from 1NF to 2NF so straightforward, it does generally reduce the amount of work to be carried out at this stage.

3NF – third normal form

In third normal form, we must ensure that no columns are dependent on other non-key attributes, often termed **transitive dependencies**. Here we have to look at both tables.

In the 'PackingNote' table, a dependency between non-key values does exist in that Customer's address is dependent on the Company name and not related to the 'NoteNo'. A similar situation exists in the 'PackingNoteItem' table where Description is dependent on the 'PartNo'.

Therefore the 3NF would consist of four tables:

- PackingNote (NoteNo, Packer, Company);
- CustomerDetail (CoName, CoAddress);
- PackingNoteItem (NoteNo, ItemNo, Qty, PartNo)
- Part (PartNo, Description).

Quick test

Describe the basic steps from un-normalised data through to third normal form.

Section 2

Anomalies

Although we have carried out the process of normalisation decanting a set of fields into a set of related tables, it still may not be entirely clear why this was done. If we use un-normalised data that does not meet 1NF, 2NF and 3NF criterian, we will encounter anomalies during processing. These can generally be broken down into three types namely **update**, **delete** and **insertion anomalies**.

Let us consider the example we used earlier. At 1NF, the table looked like Table 5.5:

Table 5.5 First normal form

NoteNo	Packer	CoName	CoAddress	ItemNo	Qty	PartNo	Desc
300	JW	Bloggs	Perth	1	200	1234	Nuts
300	JW	Bloggs	Perth	2	200	2234	Bolts
300	JW	Bloggs	Perth	3	200	3334	Washers

Note we have used the composite key NoteNo, ItemNo to ensure each entry is unique.

Update anomaly

Information about the Packer, CoName and CoAddress has been repeated in more than one row. If the CoAddress changed, then we would need to update the table with this information. Updating only one row will result in address confusion – one record would say one place while another said something else. This is termed an update anomaly. In 3NF, this cannot happen as there is one entry where the particular CoAddress for Bloggs would be stored.

Delete anomaly

Assume that Bloggs was the only company to have purchased Washers and then only once on the above packing note. If we later cancelled down the packing note then the Desc and PartNo fields would also be lost.

Insert anomaly

This is the opposite to the Delete anomaly in that we cannot establish either PartNo or Desc until we have a Packing note. To enter this information without a Packing note would result in having to enter nulls into a primary key, which is not allowed.

Quick test

What do we mean by update, delete and insert anomalies?

Section 3

Summary

Normalisation is one of the most important areas in relational databases and something that you must work to understand. There is also a clear link between ER modelling and what happens during the process of normalisation. The result of optimisation is to achieve a database which minimises redundancy and minimises the overall size of the database, and in so doing generally results in a much faster, more responsive database system that is relatively easy to maintain. It also ensures that we do not have any update, delete or insert anomalies.

Section 4

End of chapter assessment

Questions

1. With regard to normalisation of relational databases, define the following states and how you would achieve them:
   a) first normal form;
   b) second normal form;
   c) third normal form.

2. Consider from Table 5.6 the data that has to be stored in a typical university or college with regard to students, courses, modules, lecturers, etc.

Table 5.6 University/college data

Student No	Name	Programme	Programme duration (yrs)	Module No	Module name	Lecturer
1002	Steve Wilson	G701	4	COF104	IT & People	Jones
				COF118	Visual Basic	Gardner
1005	Jane Carr	G504	3	COF105	Web Basics	Smith
				COF118	Visual Basic	Gardner
				COF120	Intro to IIS	Walker
1006	Paul Carson	G701	4	COF111	Network Conf	Jones
				COF113	Intro to SE	Fish
1010	Amy Hoe	G722	2	COF111	Network Conf	Jones
				COF105	Web Basics	Smith

Essentially, a student is enrolled onto a programme and may take several modules as part of this programme. We can assume here that a module is only delivered by one lecturer. What we want to create is 1NF, 2NF and 3NF.

Answers

1. a) A relation is said to be in first normal form (1NF) if it has no repeating groups and no multi-valued attributes.
   b) A relation is said to be in second normal form (2NF) if every non-key attribute depends fully on the primary key.
   c) A relation is said to be in third normal form (3NF) if there are no dependencies on non-key fields

2. The primary key for this data would be 'Student No'. Student 'Name' could also have been a primary key except for the fact that names are not always unique. All too often we find that two students can have identical names (often in the same class). 'Student No' is always a safer approach as the registration department has access to a much greater set of data and can allocate a unique 'Student No' accordingly.

   The table clearly shows that the fields Module, Module name and Lecturer form a repeating group for a single value of 'Student No'.

   1NF – first normal form
   To go to 1NF, we will therefore split the table into two parts:

   - (Student No, Student Name, Programme, Programme Duration);
   - (Student No, Module No, Module Name, Lecturer).

   Note that 'Student No' is an acceptable key for the non-repeating portion of the table. The second table requires the use of a composite key this time using both 'Student No' and 'Module No' to uniquely identify a row of data.

   2NF – second normal form
   To move to second normal form, we are interested in the removal of partial dependencies. As the first table has no composite key, then it cannot contain partial dependencies and hence we can say that this is currently in 2NF:

   - (Student No, Student Name, Programme, Programme Duration).

   The second table does contain partial dependencies that need to be eliminated. In this case both 'Module Name' and 'Lecturer' are dependent on the 'Module No' and not the 'Student No'. To eliminate this dependency, we can again split the second table to form:

   - (Student No, Module No);
   - (Module No, Module Name, Lecturer).

   3NF – third normal form
   To move to third normal form we must remove any transitive dependencies, i.e. fields that are dependent on non-key fields.

   There is one such dependency in the first relationship where Programme 'Duration' depends on the Programme and not on the primary key 'Student No'.

   We can therefore express 3NF as follows:

   - Student (Student No, Student Name, Programme);
   - Programme (Programme, Programme Duration);
   - Student-Module (Student No, Module No);
   - Module (Module No, Module Name, Lecturer).

Chapter 6
Creating a database using Microsoft Access

Chapter summary

Having gone through much of the theory associated with relational databases, it is now time to consider the implementation of a database using a commercial DBMS. For the purposes of this book, we have chosen to use Microsoft Access due to its wide acceptance and deployment as part of Microsoft's Office Suite.

Databases can be for individual or network use. In this chapter we will look at the single user approach but in later chapters we will discuss various ways of implementing a client/server approach.

Microsoft Access is typical of many relational database products. As well as a means of maintaining an integrated set of tables and relationships, Microsoft Access allows the user to build up a set of queries, forms, reports, macros and modules. In this chapter we will explore primarily the means of both creating a database as well as entering data.

Learning outcomes

After studying this chapter, you should check your knowledge against the outcomes below and test your achievement by answering the questions at the end of the chapter. You should be able to:

Outcome 1: Understand field data types available in Microsoft Access.
You should be able to appreciate how tighter error checking can be achieved on input data through the use of data types. You should also understand the role of the null value within a database system.

Outcome 2: Understand what an index is and when you would use one.
Indexes are an integral part of relational database systems and accredited with much of its success. You should understand the different types of indexes and why these are required.

Outcome 3: Construct a basic database using Access.
You should be able to construct basic tables for a list of fields and data types, set up relationships between entities and enforce referential integrity as well as create basic and complex forms (including subforms) for data entry.

How will you be assessed on this?

This chapter has been laid out as a tutorial as much of the content will not appear in tests or exams but more likely in assignments and projects. You are actively encouraged to experiment as you work through the tutorial to see what other facilities you can intuitively use while constructing a project. Remember Microsoft Access provides a fairly comprehensive product help system which can get you out of most of the difficulties you might end up in. Frequent saves are always recommended.

One area that is likely to come up in an exam, however, is questions related to data types and the significance of the null value.

Section 1

Data types

Before proceding too far into a specific DBMS, it is worth considering why data types are important to us and what data types are generally available. Data types are convenient for many reasons such as:

- much tighter error checking on the input data;
- the ability to use mathematical operations on items of data;
- automatic formatting of data;
- more efficient memory storage;
- faster processing of queries.

We could easily store dates as text strings but this would make errors such as '32nd Geb 19876' difficult to locate and deal with. It is much better to highlight such errors at the point of data entry when it can be checked than to suffer compromising the integrity of the database. By declaring a field as a date, not only will the Month name be checked but also the existence of such a date within the specified Month/Year.

If we are planning to compute, say, an average salary of a group of employees stored in a database, then clearly knowing that the original data was available in, say, a currency field makes subsequent computation much simpler. Although conversion from one data type to another can be relatively straightforward, it is often tedious and time-consuming within the context of a DBMS.

Most DBMS contain as a minimum the following data types:

Numeric data

These are numbers that represent a value. There will be many different data types in this category varying in both their scale and precision. Databases need to be able to store small integers such as the number of people in a room through to very large integers such as the population of a continent. It needs to store real numbers such as the diameter of a hydrogen atom through to large quantities such as the diameter of a solar constellation. It must provide a means of storing fixed digit storage such as my daughter's pocket-money allowance through to the details of the US national debt (no guesses as to which is the larger!).

Strings of digits

These are numbers that do not specifically represent a value. Examples would include telephone numbers, social security numbers, etc. Entering these as numeric values would lose leading zeros as these are not considered as important in the context of numeric data. Hence storing a telephone number such as 01415675678 would end up being stored as 1415675678.

Storing numbers as text would certainly get over this issue but would not be so tight in error checking. Also another issue arises here related to sort order. If a range of numbers were stored as text, then the sort order would be as follows:

1, 10, 11, 12, 2, 23, 6, 87, 9, etc.

While on the surface this may not appear to be a major difficulty, it does make searches more difficult. For example, if you were to query the above data and request data that is less than 23, i.e. <23, the result would be:

1, 10, 11, 12, 2

Not quite what you might be expecting! Using 'Strings of Digits', the sort order would be as you expected, i.e.

1, 2, 6, 9, 10, 11, 12, 23, 87, etc.

and a query of <23 would result in

1, 2, 6, 9, 10, 11, 12

Text
Text fields allow the use of ASCII text up to the maximum field size. It is always a good idea to keep the field size as small as possible to ensure the database is not bloated unnecessarily and to keep query/search time to a minimum.

Dates
Date fields generally will allow date entry in a variety of formats according to the computer's locale settings. Not only does this data type check for valid formatting, it will also check to see that the actual date exists (checks leap year, etc.). Date fields are also important within queries either to check the difference between two dates or to establish the elapse time between a date and today's date.

Logical values
Logical (or Boolean) values store one of two values such as true/false, on/off, yes/no, etc. Generally it takes up much less storage than its equivalent character storage.

Auto number
Generally used to provide a unique field in situations where no other sensible primary key is possible.

The null value

Another important concept at this stage is that of the **null value**. This has special meaning within the context of a database. Null stands for no entry. It is not zero or blank, both of which may in fact be valid entries depending on the context. It simply signifies that an entry has not yet been made. Databases hold information we wish to collect. But what happens if the data is not available at the time of data entry? Certainly some items of data must exist for a record to exist at all (such as the primary key). Other items of data may be purely informational and optional to the existence of a record. In order to allow a record to be stored, the database can maintain a placeholder using a null without implying any meaning behind this data value.

Nulls mean different things in different contexts. For example, a database may store the date a person is married. Whether this implies that every person in the database has to get married depends on the database in question. In the case of a record of job applicants, it might simply imply that the person was not married at the time of applying for a job. Alternatively if the database concerned a marriage allowance, it may mean that the wedding date was not at hand when the record was entered.

Nulls are used for any data type and hence cannot be used as a search criterion across different columns. In other words a null in one column cannot be compared or equated to a null in a different column. It is also true that nulls cannot be compared to any other value. This may throw up some odd situations at times which should be understood. For example, if a search was made to find all rows where a column was equal to a specific value, then the database would return a certain number of records. Simply negating the criterion would yield a search to find all rows where a column was not equal to a specific value. The sum of the two queries would not add up to the total number of records if that particular column contained nulls. This makes sense in that at the time of making the query, nothing is actually known of the entries which contain null and therefore cannot be said to fit into either query.

Finally, nulls used in calculations result in null values. Again this makes sense in that if you were to, say, multiply an unknown by 12, then the result must also be unknown.

Available data types in Access 2002 (distributed as part of Office XP)

Like most commercial database products, Microsoft Access 2002 has a rich set of data types (see Table 6.1).

Table 6.1 Microsoft Access 2002 data types

Data type	Size	Used for
Text	Up to 255 characters	Used for text, for a combination of text and numbers or for numbers that do not require calculation, e.g. phone numbers, part numbers, etc.
Memo	Up to 65,536 characters	Used for lengthy text such as notes, descriptions, etc.
Number	Up to 8 bytes	Any numerical value (except currency).
Date/time	8 bytes	Used to store date/time. Access stores dates internally as a number. For a date, this represents the number of elapsed days since 31 December 1899.
Currency	8 bytes	Currency values are stored at a higher than normal precision to prevent rounding off errors when used in calculations.
Auto number	4 bytes	Generates unique sequential or random integer numbers. Often used as a primary key where no other values are available in the other fields.
Yes/no	1 bit	Contains one of two values, either yes/no or true/false or on/off, etc. Null is not allowed in this type of field.
OLE object	Up to 1 gigabyte	OLE objects created in other applications such as bitmaps, sounds, etc.
Hyperlink	Up to 64,000 characters	Used for hyperlinks to URLs or valid UNC path.
Lookup wizard	Typically 4 bytes	Use to create a field that allows selection from another table or combo box,

Within the concept of a number, Access supports the number types listed in Table 6.2 through its field size property.

Table 6.2 Microsoft Access 2002 number types

Number type	Range of values	Decimal precision	Size
Byte	0 to 255	None	1 byte
Decimal	-10^{28} through to $+10^{28}$	28	12 bytes
Integer	$-32,768$ to $+32,767$	None	2 bytes
Long integer	$-2,147,483,648$ to $+2,147,483,647$	None	4 bytes
Single	-3.4×10^{38} to $+3.4 \times 10^{38}$	7	4 bytes
Double	-1.797×10^{308} to $+1.797 \times 10^{308}$	15	8 bytes

Quick test

What is the primary function of using different data types within a database?

Section 2

Purpose and use of database indexes

Indexes within databases provide essentially the same function as they do within a book or other record-keeping scheme. They provide a fast, efficient and scalable means of accessing and retrieving data. Indeed, it is this feature alone that arguably accounts for the phenomenal success of the relational database. Prior to the use of indexes, databases had used navigational techniques such as linked lists where one record would point to the next record which in turn would point to the next, etc. If two-directional navigation was required then double linked lists were often used with each record holding a pointer to not only the next record but also the previous record.

The B-tree indexing system dramatically changed the way data could be accessed. Consider the possible stored values shown in Table 6.3.

Table 6.3 Stored values

Physical record	AccountNo	Name	Location
1	A1002	Peterson	Belfast
2	A1004	Brown	London
3	B1123	James	Coventry
4	A1003	Anderson	Belfast
5	C1233	Jack	Cardiff
6	B1022	Stevens	London
7	A1000	Dennison	Glasgow

Note that the number at the left-hand side of the table indicates the order the data is stored in rather than a separate field. AccountNo has been nominated as the primary key.

Databases such as Microsoft Access support two types of indexes, namely a **unique index** or a **non-unique index**. A unique index does not allow duplicate values within a column. A non-unique index supports duplicate values within a column. Primary key fields, for example, use a unique index. In fact, in databases such as Access, the primary key index is automatically built so you do not need to request this.

Keys can be single columns or multiple columns; here we have specified a single key column AccountNo. This would yield Table 6.4.

Table 6.4

AccountNo	Record
A1000	7
A1002	1
A1003	4
A1004	2
B1022	6
B1123	3
C1233	5

To access a record, we simply look up the index and immediately proceed to that particular record.

Consider now what would happen if we created an index based on the column 'Name'. This would yield Table 6.5.

Table 6.5

Name	Record
Anderson	4
Brown	2
Dennison	7
Jack	5
James	3
Peterson	1
Stevens	6

Clearly here we have a different means of accessing a record based on 'Name'.

Building a table based on Town, however, highlights a slightly different situation as shown in Table 6.6.

Here we can see clearly why we need the ability to build non-unique indexes.

How many indexes can we have?

Well clearly a great deal, but is it a good idea to construct indexes out of everything in sight just in case we might wish to use it later in a query? The answer to that is 'no' but for reasons not related directly to querying. Indexes have to be maintained

Table 6.6

Town	Record
Belfast	1, 4
Cardiff	5
Coventry	3
Glasgow	7
London	2, 6

in order to be useful. There is no point in looking up an index only to find that record 6 has been changed and data now resides in record 12987. Every time we change the order of a record (which could apply at any update), all related indexes have to change. The more the indexes, the more changes will be required. Updating indexes results in an increase in hard disk activity which may soon get to a stage where the overall database performance was being hampered by the process of updating the indexes.

Databases such as Access have their own internal rules for creating indexes if you use some of the wizard tools within Access. However, occasionally you do come across strange rules where indexes get created even without wizards and without you even asking. For example, if you are creating a new table in Design view, any fields whose name ends in ID are automatically marked for the creation of an index.

Quick test

What is the main disadvantage of creating too many indexes (i.e. more than you are likely to use)?

Section 3

Building an Access database

As we will find later, Microsoft Access has several means of interacting with its DBMS. Roughly these break down into three areas:

- visual programming techniques – this will be explored in both this and the succeeding chapter;
- via a software programming interface such as ADO, ODBC, RDO, etc. – this will be covered in Chapter 10;
- via an SQL interface – this we will explore in Chapter 12.

For now we will use Access as a stand-alone program on a single PC.

Let's create a simple database system to monitor sales of PC components to a group of customers. In terms of design we will consider the ER diagram in Figure 6.1.

A customer receives one or more than one invoice for goods bought, an invoice can have one or more line items, a line item can be used for one or more items of stock.

The object is to create the following:

- four tables (Customer, Invoice, LineItem and Stock);
- three forms – the first to enter customer data, the second to enter available stock data and the third to enter a sales invoice;

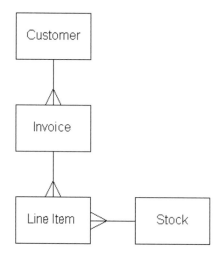

Figure 6.1 ER diagram

- one query – build a sales query to show summary sales information;
- one report – design a sales by customer report.

This has been written as a tutorial session but will contain areas where you will be expected to produce additional work on your own.

First we need to map out the fields, data types and keys for all four tables. These will be as follows.

Table 6.7

Customer

Field name	Data type	Field size	Comments
CustomerID	Text	6	Primary key
FirstName	Text	15	
LastName	Text	20	
Address1	Text	20	
Address2	Text	20	
TownCity	Text	15	
Region	Text	15	
PostCode	Text	8	
CreditLimit	Currency		
Balance	Currency		

Table 6.8

Invoice

Field name	Data type	Field size	Comments
InvoiceNo	Number	Integer	Primary key
InvDate	Date/Time	Short Date	
CustomerID	Text	6	
SalesStaff	Text	3	

Table 6.9

LineItem

Field name	Data type	Field size	Comments
InvoiceNo	Number	Integer	Primary key
ItemNo	Text	10	Primary key
SalesPrice	Currency		
NumUnits	Number	Integer	

Table 6.10

Stock

Field name	Data type	Field size	Comments
ItemNo	Text	10	Primary key
Description	Text	30	
UnitCost	Currency		
UnitPrice	Currency		
UnitsOrdered	Number	Integer	
UnitsInStock	Number	Integer	

Having previously installed the software, Access can be started by clicking on the Microsoft Access icon on the Start|Programs menu. (Microsoft Access 2002 was used during development of this book but the exercises will support previous versions of Access from Access 97.) The opening screen shown in Figure 6.2 is revealed.

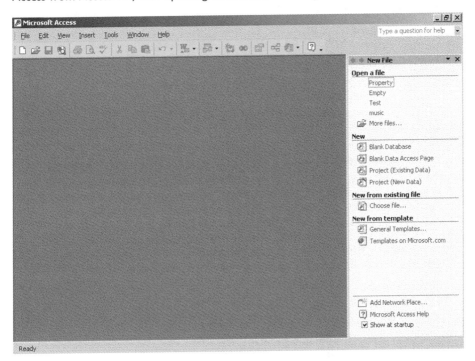

Figure 6.2 Microsoft Access: opening screen

As we are creating a new database, select 'blank database' from the list presented on the right of the screen. You will be asked for a database filename (suggest using 'Trader') after which Access will leave the environment in table view as in Figure 6.3.

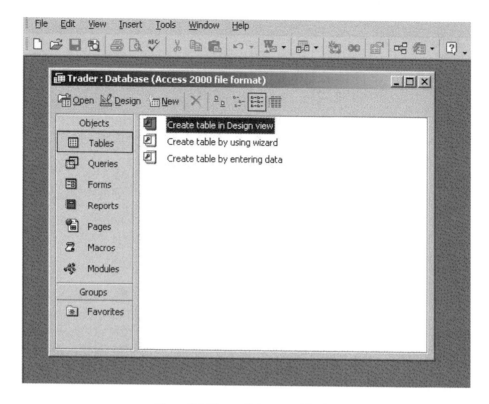

Figure 6.3 Microsoft Access: table view

Take a few minutes to familiarise yourself with this environment as it is the heart of Access's user interface. At this point, Access allows you to create several types of objects such as Tables, Queries, Forms, Reports, Pages, Macros and Modules. Access saves any object you create in one file giving it an extension '.mdb'. Each separate database takes up a different file with all information necessary (including your data) stored within this file.

This is completely different from some other DBMS systems such as Oracle. With Oracle, as a user you have access to a certain storage area generally called your database. It is not one file but a collection of files each one having a purpose within your 'space'. Indeed, with systems such as Oracle, if you have designed several database systems, then it is likely that tables from both systems are stored side by side on your hard drive necessitating that all table names be unique. Under Microsoft Access, different systems could have the same table names. This is not ambiguous as the system will use the tables stored within its own '.mdb' file.

Let us return to the tutorial. Select the icon 'Create Table in Design View' and start to fill in the fields for the first table 'Customer' (see Figure 6.4).

The pane on the lower half of the window allows customisation of the data type – in the above case note that the field size has been reduced to 6 characters in line with our earlier data type design specification. Access allows a high degree of customisation including input masks, individual field validation rules, whether or not an entry is required, etc. For now we will accept the defaults.

After the data for each field has been entered and the data checked, it is important to mark the primary key field(s). To do this simply highlight one or more fields and depress the 'key' icon. This places a small key next to the field name(s). If you do not specify a primary key field, the software will ask during the save cycle.

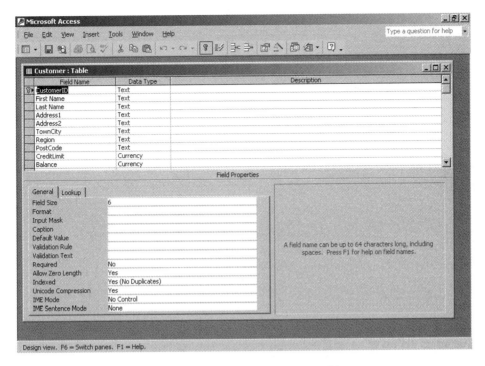

Figure 6.4 Microsoft Access: create table

When all is complete simply close down the table details by clicking the X box at the top right-hand side of the Table entry screen. Access will then prompt for a table name in which it will store the information.

On your own now, enter in table data for Invoice, Line Item and Stock using the table data listed earlier.

After this process is complete for all tables, it is time to specify the relationships between fields in the various tables. This is done by selecting Relationships from the Tools menu. You will be prompted to select the various tables you would wish to relate. In this case you should choose all the tables by selecting each table in turn. Access places a representation of each table in the Relationships pane. Provided your screen resolution allows, it is worthwhile resizing these tables to show all fields.

Your task now will be to describe the relationships to Access by selecting a particular field, dragging it across the pane and dropping it onto its related field. As an example select 'CustomerID' in the Customer table and drag this onto the 'Cus-tomerID' field in the Invoice table. Immediately a dialogue box as shown in Figure 6.5 opens up to get further information of the relationship.

Select 'Enforce Referential Integrity' and complete the process by depressing the 'OK' button. This will then show the resulting relationship between the two tables in the Relationships pane as a one-to-many relationship.

Complete on your own the following relationships:

- InvoiceNo in Invoice table to InvoiceNo in the LineItem table;
- ItemNo in LineItem table to ItemNo in the Stock table.

This should now leave the relationships displayed as in Figure 6.6.

Note that it is always worthwhile moving the entities around the relationship pane to try and get a simplified view of the relationships. You may wish to print out a

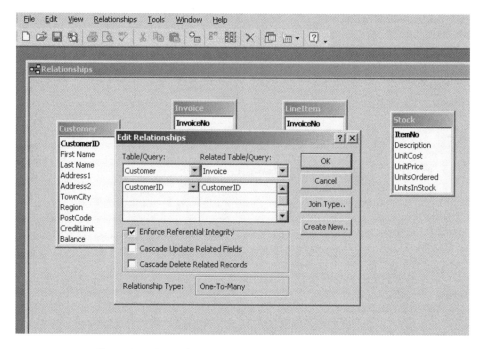

Figure 6.5 Microsoft Access: relationship information request

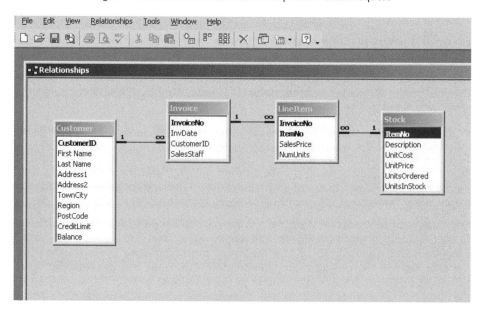

Figure 6.6 Microsoft Access: completed relationships pane

copy of the relationships table as this not only gives the relationships but also a useful list of all fields used in the database.

Close the relationships pane (after saving).

Having built up the tables and created the relationships, it is now time to enter some data. Double clicking on any of the tables we have created will allow us to enter data directly into the database. While this is good for developers, it is not particularly user friendly. It would be much better to create a set of well laid-out forms which closely mimic the way data arrives to allow us to carry out the data entry phase in a more natural way.

As we stated at the start of this tutorial, we have opted to develop three forms to take care of the likely tasks within our system. The first would be to add to or update our customer data. The second would allow us to add to or update our current stock. The third will be used to enter customer purchases at the time of purchase.

First select Forms as an object in the main Access user interface. This should show two available options, namely

- Create Form from Design view;
- Create Form Using Wizard.

Creating a form in Design View is a tedious process as compared to making use of the Form Wizard. In any event we will end up manually tidying up the form in Design View.

Click on the Forms tab and select 'Create Form by Using Wizard'. Highlight the Customer Table and select the fields we wish to include on the form. In this case we will be choosing all the fields. Access allows you to select individual fields by either double clicking the appropriate field or highlighting the field and depressing the '>' button. Alternatively you can select all fields by depressing the '>>' button. Note that as each field is selected, it becomes unavailable for selection again. If a mistake is made, then the same mechanism allows for deselection of either individual or all fields using the '<' or '<<' buttons.

With all fields selected, press the next button and select a 'Columnar' layout followed by the selection of a 'Standard Style'. Access provides a whole host of possible combinations of Layout and Style but for the purposes of this exercise we will restrict it to Columnar and Standard style. You will then be prompted for a Form Name which we will call 'Customer Input Form'. Finally select 'Modify the Forms Design' before you click finish – this will take you directly to the Design View. If you didn't select the modify form radio button, do not worry. Simply highlight the Customer Input Form and select Design View from the menu immediately above.

Access then creates the form in Design View. In this view, fields can be moved, captions renamed, font sizes changed, graphics introduced, etc. You should also notice that there are three sections to the form – a form header, form detail and the form footer. Both the header and the footer are common areas that will display the same information on all forms. The detail area changes for each entry. Expand the Form Header Section by pointing the mouse to the area between Detail and Form Header. When the icon changes from the arrow, select the left-hand mouse button and drag the detail section downwards to give sufficient space to the form header.

The toolbox provides a selection of Windows controls to enhance the layout. If this does not appear as either a 'floating' or 'docked' menu (see Figure 6.7), then select Toolbox from the upper View menu. In this case we will simply use the Label control (marked 'Aa' in the Toolbox) to create a title. Select and drag the mouse across a suitable area of the form header to mark out an area and type in the required text

Figure 6.7 Toolbox as docked menu

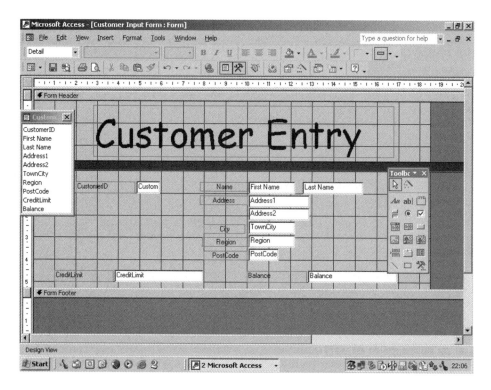

Figure 6.8 Microsoft Access: form header

(in this case Customer Entry). The font can be changed in style, colour, font size, etc. to create the desired effect (see Figure 6.8).

In the detail part of the form, it is often advantageous to regroup the fields on a more logical basis. During the form creation process Access creates both fields and captions. It then binds these two items together such that if you move one you will also move the other. This may not be what you desire. Access does, however, give you the ability to move each independently of each other by selecting the larger 'handle' at the top left of the control although in many cases it is more convenient to delete the label and recreate this at a later date.

CRUCIAL TIP

Although Access automatically sets the size of the text boxes to match the data widths it is expecting, you may find that some adjustment may be necessary when you come to entering data if you wish to see the whole data. Simply go into Design View for the form and adjust the **field width** as appropriate.

CRUCIAL TIP

Depending on how the various fields were moved around the form, it may be necessary to adjust the tab order of the fields. It is customary in Windows to move from one field to the next depressing the Tab key. Tab order can be adjusted by 'right-clicking' anywhere on the form area and selecting '**Tab Order**', following the instructions provided.

When you are happy with your new form simply close the form, saving it with a suitable title such as 'Customer Input Form'. Double clicking the newly created form name will then open up the form in data entry mode as in Figure 6.9.

You should now develop the 'Stock' form on the same basis.

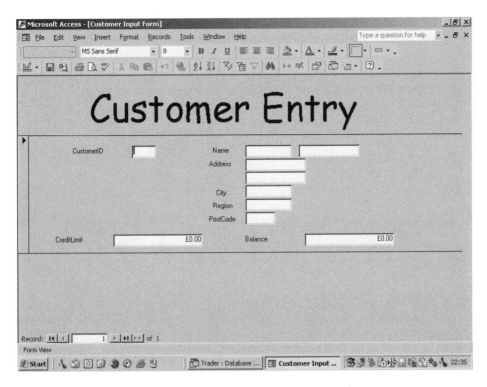

Figure 6.9 Microsoft Access: data entry mode

Both these forms are in themselves straightforward as the fields come directly from only one table. On a similar basis, we could prepare input forms for both the Invoice and the LineItem tables but this would not be good practice. User interface should follow as closely as possible the real-life events – we should not be forcing real-life events to follow the physical mapping of a relational database. The DBMS has to be strong and robust enough to take care of these issues.

As we have previously commented, Customer Entry and Stock Entry tables closely follow real-life events. In the case of Customer Entry, the whole form relates to a single customer, the data for which would likely come from the same source – perhaps an application for an account facility. Issues such as credit limit would be determined on either the requested credit or from the customer's perceived creditworthiness. In a similar fashion, information relating to stock would also likely come from one source, perhaps the supplier's invoices. The Unit Price would likely be a policy decision based on experience and knowledge of the marketplace. For argument's sake here we have applied a 30 per cent profit margin to all non-cable products and 25 per cent on all cable products.

An example of the Stock Entry form is shown in Figure 6.10.

When developing database applications, it is often helpful to have data available during development that can be used to test out various features. The data shown in Figure 6.11 should be keyed in using the Customer Entry form.

In a similar manner, key in the information shown in Figure 6.12 via the Stock Entry form.

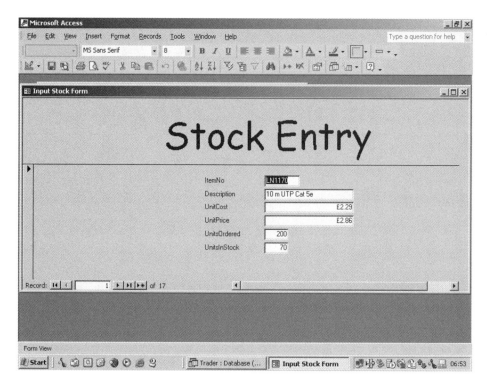

Figure 6.10 Microsoft Access: stock entry form

		CustomerID	First Name	Last Name	Address1	Address2
▶	+	cevens	Charles	Evans	21 Hill Street	Grangetown
	+	cpark	Chris	Park	12 Spring Lane	Gosforth
	+	csmith	Colin	Smith	23 David Drive	
	+	gblack	George	Black	32 Dyer Lane	Pepperton
	+	jjones	Janice	Jones	15 High Street	Riverdale
	+	mbruce	Mary	Bruce	11 Dolfin Drive	Hillend

Record: ◀◀ ◀ | 1 | ▶ ▶◀ ▶* of 6

TownCity	Region	PostCode	CreditLimit	Balance
Sunderland	Tyne & Wear	SR2 9EH	£30,000.00	£23.97
Newcastle	Tyne & Wear	NE4 9HT	£3,000.00	£97.29
Cardiff	Wales	CF10 7XD	£15,000.00	£34.42
St Albans	Hertfordshire	AL4 6CL	£12,000.00	£345.78
Lewisham	London	SE6 8ER	£1,500.00	£567.34
Stirling	Central Region	FK9 4JH	£50,000.00	£0.00
			£0.00	£0.00

Figure 6.11 Customer entry form

ItemNo	Description	UnitCost	UnitPrice	UnitsOrdered	UnitsInStock
LN1170	10 m UTP Cat 5e	£2.29	£2.86	200	70
LN1173	20 m UTP Cat 5e	£4.10	£5.13	0	95
LN1376	1 Port Print Server	£58.75	£76.38	0	12
LN1378	3 Port Print Server	£75.79	£98.53	0	23
LN2559	24 Port 10/100 Switch	£115.15	£149.70	5	1
LN3393	1 m UTP Cat 5e	£0.82	£1.03	100	67
LN3922	32 Port 10/100 Switch	£157.45	£204.69	0	10
LN3942	HP DeskJet D-155xi	£500.55	£650.78	5	0
LN4108	Sony Vaio FX-705	£1,382.98	£1,797.87	0	5
LN4139	HP DeskJet 5550c	£137.48	£178.72	0	4
LN4248	HP DeskJet 3420	£57.58	£74.85	0	9
LN4352	Sony Vaio FX-802	£1,039.88	£1,351.84	0	3
LN4353	Sony Vaio FX-805	£1,323.23	£1,720.20	0	6
LN4354	Sony Vaio FX-801	£856.58	£1,113.54	0	12
LN4355	Sony Vaio SRX 51PA	£1,702.99	£2,213.89	0	4
LN4478	HP DeskJet 3325	£45.82	£59.57	0	2
LN726	16 Port 10/100 Switch	£55.81	£72.55	0	8
		£0.00	£0.00	0	0

Record: 1 of 17

Figure 6.12 Stock entry data

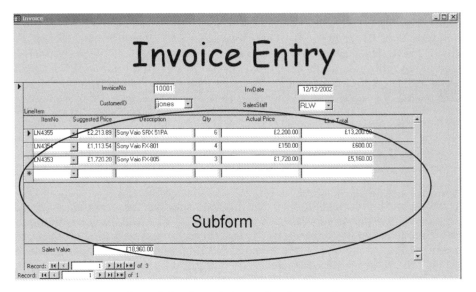

Figure 6.13 Microsoft Access: invoice entry form

Invoice entry

For the Invoice Entry screen, we need a wholly different approach. As much of the data pre-exists, such as CustomerID, ItemNo and descriptions, it is important that we type in only what we have to and either select from options or use calculated fields for the balance. Let us look first at the finished Invoice Entry form shown in Figure 6.13.

The first thing you may notice about this form that is different from the previous two forms is that there appears to be two sets of records, one nested inside the other. This is indeed the reality of the situation where we have an invoice LineItem object embedded inside an Invoice item. Let us take them one at a time.

Invoice entry form

First create a new form using the wizard. You are then requested for fields to be included in the form. Select all fields in the Invoice table and proceed on the same basis as the previous two forms. Once the wizard is complete, open up the form in Design View and create title 'Invoice Entry' in the form header.

In the form Detail section, lay out the controls to match that shown in Figure 6.13. Now we stated at the start of this section that we do not want to have to retype data that should already be available. In the case of 'CustomerID', we already have stored in the Customer table all available 'CustomerIDs'. We also created a relationship between 'CustomerID' in the Invoice table and 'CustomerID' in the Customer table. This means that we can get Access to give a list of all possible 'CustomerIDs' without having to type it out and risk an error. First we need to delete the text box (and associated label) created by the form wizard, then create a combo box by selecting this on the Toolbox and dragging the mouse across the form to set its dimensions. Access will launch its Combo Box Wizard dialogue.

CRUCIAL TIP

If the Combo Box Wizard dialogue does not launch, it is because you do not have the 'Control Wizards' button selected in the toolbar. Simply select the toolbar button with the magic wand and repeat this process:

In this case select 'I want the combo box to look up the values in a table or query' and press next. Select Table: Customer followed by 'CustomerID' field on the next screen. The wizard gives you a chance to adjust the field width. In the next screen we need to bind this data to the control by selecting 'Store that value in this field' and selecting 'CustomerID'. Lastly we get the chance to set the control label – in this case 'CustomerID' is good. You will likely need to readjust the width of the combo box.

CRUCIAL TIP

It is also good practice to rename the combo box 'CustomerID' (not just the Control Name) as it can be very confusing when adjusting the tab order at a later stage. To change the control name, right click on the combo box and select the 'All' tab.

In the case of the 'SalesStaff' field, this was specified as a three-letter code (presumably the person's initials). As the number of staff will likely be reasonably well fixed, it would be also good to replace the textbox with a combo box. In this case, after the combo box is created and the Combo Box Wizard appears, select 'I will type the values that I want'. Access then presents a small spreadsheet to accept manual values – use RLW, JCB, RMT, JJS (or any other three letter combinations you wish). In the next screen, remember to select 'Store that value in this field' and select 'SalesStaff' from the list. As before you will be given the chance to set an appropriate control label ('SalesStaff') – also do not forget to change the name of the control through the properties command.

It is worth while saving the design and double clicking the Invoice Form to see how the form looks. At this stage you should recognise a form which correctly displays all available customers in the 'CustomerID' combo box as well as already knows your Sales Staff in an appropriate combo box.

Creation of subform

To create a subform, first open back up the Invoice Entry in Design mode. You may well need to open up further the detail section to accept the subform.

Table 6.11 Subform fields

Table	Field
LineItem	Item
Stock	UnitPrice
Stock	Description
LineItem	NumUnits
LineItem	SalesPrice

From the Toolbox, select Subform/SubReport control. Drag this over a suitable area in the Detail section of the form. Access then opens up the SubForm Wizard. Select 'Use existing Tables and Queries' and in the next screen select all the fields you wish to appear in the subform. In our case, this should consist of the fields listed in Table 6.11.

Next select 'Choose from list' accepting the default and lastly accept the suggested name for the subform (LineItem Subform).

It is again worthwhile saving this form as it stands and double click on Invoice Entry Form. Clearly we are making progress but there are still a few matters to be tidied up.

Close the form and open up the LineItem Subform in Design mode. From the Toolbox, add a textbox after SalesPrice. Select this textbox, right click the mouse and select Properties, depressing the 'All' tab. Change the Name to 'LineTotal'. Next select the Control Source entry. Both an arrow and three dots will appear at the end of the line. Selecting the three dots takes you to the Expression Builder dialogue. Dialogue boxes use the actual objects to create an expression relieving you of the burden of spelling, etc. First hit the '=' button then open up the Forms|Loaded Forms|LineItem subform folders in the left-hand pane. Select 'SalesPrice' followed by the '*' multiply operator followed by 'NumUnits'. Finally hit the 'OK' button. This stores the expression built in the Control Source section of the properties.

Staying in the properties box, we need to change the format to 'Currency' and the Locked property to 'Yes' to make sure that this is a calculated field and not one which will accept an entry. Close the properties dialogue. Change the label for this control to read 'LineTotal'.

Until now we have been using Access Datasheet display for display of the subform. However, this will not allow us to see headers or footers. In our case we would like to display a total Invoice value in the footer of the subform. However, this is easy to change. Load the 'LineItem' subform in Design View. Carefully delete all field labels in the Detail section without removing the actual fields (highlight the large square handle on the text label and press delete. If you accidentally take out a field then press Control-Z to undo). Next move the fields into one line along the top of the Detail section, being careful to maintain the correct order (you may need to adjust the width of the fields as appropriate). Next reduce the size of the Detail section to a minimum by moving the Footer bar.

While we are at this stage, it is also worthwhile deleting the 'ItemNo' textbox and replacing this with a combo box of the same name. This will make things much easier to enter. At the Combo Box Wizard, select 'I want the combo box to look up the values in a table or query', select the Stock table, the 'ItemNo' field and store this in the field called 'ItemNo'.

Open up both the Header bar and Footer bar. Place a series of labels in the Header section and line these up with the fields in the Detail section. Give appropriate column headers to these labels. In the Footer section, open up a Textbox changing its label to 'SalesValue'. Next select the textbox, right click and choose properties, pressing the 'All' tab. Change the name to 'SalesValue'. In the Control Source, build up the expression

=Sum([SalesPrice]*[NumUnits])

Next, select the small black spot at the top left-hand corner of the form, press the right-hand mouse button and select Properties. Change the default View to be 'Continuous Forms'. Save the LineItem subform and exit.

Finally we must set the properties of the 'read-only' fields to Locked=Yes. The fields in question are

- Unit Price (read-only from the Stock table);
- Description (read-only from the Stock table).

If you do not set these to Locked, then entering data at these fields would overwrite the respective tables. Also take the opportunity to set the Format property of this field to 'Currency'.

Save your work, then double click the Invoice Entry form to start data entry.

Data entry

You are obviously free to enter as much data as you choose in order to create a basis for reports in the next section. As a minimum you are requested to enter in the following invoices in Figures 6.14 and 6.15 using the Invoice Entry form which we can pick up on again later.

InvoiceNo	InvDate	CustomerID	SalesStaff
10001	09/08/2002	jjones	RLW
10002	10/08/2002	cpark	JCB
10003	11/08/2002	gblack	JJS
10004	12/08/2002	mbruce	RLW
10005	13/08/2002	cpark	JJS
10006	14/08/2002	cevens	JCB
10007	15/08/2002	csmith	JJS
10008	16/08/2002	jjones	JCB
10009	17/08/2002	mbruce	RLW
10010	18/08/2002	gblack	JCB

Figure 6.14 Invoice table

Indexes

Before we conclude this tutorial, it is worth picking up the issue we discussed earlier in the chapter on the subject of indexes. Open the various tables up in Design view and check which fields Access has created an index for and which fields it hasn't. Try to work out why some are created and some not, bearing in mind the earlier comments in this chapter.

InvoiceNo	ItemNo	SalesPrice	NumUnits
10001	LN4353	£1,720.20	3
10001	LN4354	£1,113.54	4
10001	LN4355	£2,213.89	6
10002	LN1378	£98.53	3
10003	LN1378	£98.53	1
10003	LN3942	£650.78	1
10004	LN1170	£2.86	100
10004	LN1173	£5.13	50
10005	LN4354	£1,113.54	1
10005	LN726	£72.55	8
10006	LN4353	£1,720.20	1
10006	LN4354	£1,113.54	1
10007	LN4248	£74.85	3
10007	LN4478	£59.57	2
10008	LN1376	£76.38	24
10008	LN2559	£149.70	12
10009	LN4139	£178.72	4
10010	LN1376	£76.38	1
10010	LN3942	£650.78	7
10010	LN4354	£1,113.54	1

Figure 6.15 Invoice item table

Section 4

Summary

The tutorial has taken you through a simple but typical design example for a small database system. You simply enter the Invoice number, the date, make a selection on an item which in turn displays both a description and suggested price. You then enter in the bought quantity and price negotiated and the system will calculate the line value. After entering all of the line items, the system will calculate the overall price. This is typical of how many traders work in that they have a recommended price but are free to negotiate discounts to certain customers.

But what else is missing? Well, it's now back to you. It would be nice to see more of the customer's details on the screen (such as full name and address). It would also be nice to see his credit limit and to tell us whether or not the sale would in fact be allowed to continue. However, it must be remembered that the current balance field is not linked to the invoices so it is only as good as the last update.

Try out these enhancements to the system and we will take up the story of queries and reports in the next chapter.

Section 5

End of chapter assessment

Questions

1. What is the significance of the null value as used within a database system?

2. List the main data types usually provided by a database system.

3. Explain the purpose of a database index and why there must be at least two types of indexes.

4. What is the prime purpose of a form within a database system?

5. Describe why tab ordering is important in the context of a database form.

Answers

1. Null is the termed used to denote that no input has been made. Where a field is mandatory, it is usual that the field is set to 'NOT NULL' or 'field required'. Primary fields cannot be null as a primary field value must be unique.

2. The main data types usually supported by a database system include:

   - text or character (alphanumeric);
   - numeric – several formats (integer or floating point);
   - date and time;
   - Boolean (true/false, on/off, yes/no, etc.);
   - counter or auto number generator.

   Be careful with this type of question as it relates to general databases and is not Microsoft specific. Fields such as OLE objects, hyperlinks and Lookup wizards are examples of vendor-specific fields.

3. An index is a look-up mechanism relating an ordered sort of one or more table columns to specific records stored within a database. It functions in a very similar manner to an index in the back of a book. At least two types of indexes are required, unique and non-unique. Unique would be used for primary key indexes whereas non-unique key indexes would be used where there was a possibility of more than one key existing within a particular column.

4. A form is a means of entering data based on how data is collected rather than how data is organised within a database. It often mimics paper-driven systems and can update more than one table from a form.

5. Tab ordering affects the next field the cursor points to when the user advances the fields by pressing the 'Tab' key. Generally the 'Enter' key is used to denote completion of the form whereas Tab advances a field within a form. Tab ordering is important as the sequence should follow the logical layout of the form and not some arbitrary table order. Incorrect tab ordering wastes time on data entry and can often lead to entry mistakes with the user anticipating where he expects the cursor to advance to.

Chapter 7
More on database management systems

Chapter summary

In this chapter we are going to build on the work of the previous chapter, this time showing more of the features of a database management system. We will start by looking at queries and reports, two of the essential means of getting organised data from a database management system.

Learning outcomes

After studying this chapter, you should check your knowledge against the outcomes below and test your achievement by answering the questions at the end of the chapter. You should be able to:

Outcome 1: Construct a query.
Queries provide a powerful way of extracting relevant data from a mass of organised data in a database. You should be able to construct various queries organising the results into a single table for subsequent actions.

Outcome 2: Construct a report.
As well as construct a report, you should be able to use data collected from a previous query to populate a report.

Outcome 3: Understand the role of the database administrator.
You should be able to appreciate one of the key database management functions within a company, namely that of the DBA which carries with it many important responsibilities.

How will you be assessed on this?

Like the last chapter it is unlikely that this material will appear in any test or exam but rather feature in an assignment or project. Again you are encouraged to experiment as you work through this tutorial making full use of the Microsoft Access help system where appropriate.

The role of the database administrator is often an essay-style exam question or is sometimes used as an assignment.

Section 1

Constructing queries

With relationships defined, you can start to build simple or complex queries. A **query** is a way of selecting, sorting and filtering data in preparation for a specific use. It is not confined to only one table – indeed, this in many ways is the power behind the query. A query can collect and sort data that meets specific criteria from different tables and present this as though it was an actual table. More importantly, as we will see, this can be used just like any other table to populate reports.

First select Queries as an object in the main Access user interface. This should show two available options, namely:

- Create Query in Design View;
- Create Query by using Wizard.

Select Create Query in Design View. Access then puts up a blank relationship window and requests you to select which tables are involved in the Query. In our case we want to select all four tables, Customer, Invoice, LineItem and Stock. After this we can close the table selection window. Access will have placed the tables in the relationship window and drawn the already established relationships.

The next task is to select what data is going to be important to the report. The report we intend to construct will be a listing of Sales by Customer. Therefore the fields we will likely require will be:

- Customer Name;
- Invoice Date;
- InvoiceNo;
- ItemNo;
- Description;
- SalesPrice;
- No of Units;
- Amount.

All these fields are directly assessable from one or another of the tables except two: Customer Name should be a concatenation of LastName and FirstName, while Amount will be a computation of the SalesPrice times No of Units.

The solution is shown in Figure 7.1.

With regard to the middle six fields in the lower pane, these are all available as existing fields within a table. Placing the cursor in the Table row produces a combo box to allow you to select the table. Similarly placing the cursor in the Field row produces a combo box to allow you to select a field within that table. If Table is not set, then the Field combo box will display all available fields. Alternatively Access allows you to select a field in the relationship window and drag this onto a Field box. Access will also correctly identify the table in question.

In the case of the first field, however, no such field (in the form we need it) exists. To get over this we simply type in the new name of the field (in this case Name) followed by a colon and the detailed expression within brackets. The Access convention for field names is to place these inside square brackets. Part of the necessity for doing this relates to the fact that Access field names can contain spaces whereas most other DBMS systems do not support spaces in field names. (This will become more evident in the later section on SQL.)

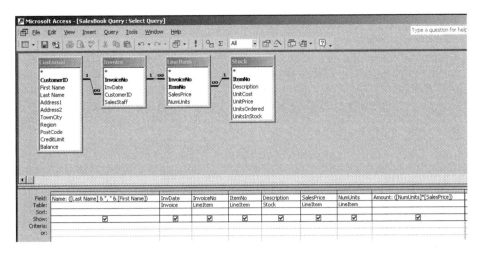

Figure 7.1 Microsoft Access: query solution

The field we wish to construct is the Last Name, followed by a comma and a space, followed by the First Name. To achieve this we use the concatenation operator '&'. In this case:

([Last Name] & "," & [First Name])

In the case of the final field, remember we did previously calculate the line item value but we did not save this. Unless necessary, it is generally good practice not to save anything you can reasonably derive at a later stage. Storing computations introduces redundancy back into the database, makes it larger and inevitably will slow it down. With the processing speed of modern computers it is an easy task to carry out a late calculation as and when required.

So what is the result of the query? Simply depress the run operator ('!') and Access produces the table shown in Figure 7.2.

Name	InvDate	InvoiceNo	ItemNo	Description	SalesPrice	NumUnits	Amount
Jones, Janice	09/08/2002	10001	LN4353	Sony Vaio FX-805	£1,720.20	3	£5,160.60
Jones, Janice	09/08/2002	10001	LN4355	Sony Vaio SRX 51PA	£2,213.89	6	£13,283.34
Jones, Janice	09/08/2002	10001	LN4354	Sony Vaio FX-801	£1,113.54	4	£4,454.16
Park, Chris	10/08/2002	10002	LN1378	3 Port Print Server	£98.53	3	£295.59
Black, George	11/08/2002	10003	LN3942	HP DeskJet D-155xi	£650.78	1	£650.78
Black, George	11/08/2002	10003	LN1378	3 Port Print Server	£98.53	1	£98.53
Bruce, Mary	12/08/2002	10004	LN1170	10 m UTP Cat 5e	£2.86	100	£286.00
Bruce, Mary	12/08/2002	10004	LN1173	20 m UTP Cat 5e	£5.13	50	£256.50
Park, Chris	13/08/2002	10005	LN726	16 Port 10/100 Switch	£72.55	8	£580.40
Park, Chris	13/08/2002	10005	LN4354	Sony Vaio FX-801	£1,113.54	1	£1,113.54
Evans, Charles	14/08/2002	10006	LN4354	Sony Vaio FX-801	£1,113.54	1	£1,113.54
Evans, Charles	14/08/2002	10006	LN4353	Sony Vaio FX-805	£1,720.20	1	£1,720.20
Smith, Colin	15/08/2002	10007	LN4248	HP DeskJet 3420	£74.85	3	£224.55
Smith, Colin	15/08/2002	10007	LN4478	HP DeskJet 3325	£59.57	2	£119.14
Jones, Janice	16/08/2002	10008	LN1376	1 Port Print Server	£76.38	24	£1,833.12
Jones, Janice	16/08/2002	10008	LN2559	24 Port 10/100 Switch	£149.70	12	£1,796.40
Bruce, Mary	17/08/2002	10009	LN4139	HP DeskJet 5550c	£178.72	4	£714.88
Black, George	18/08/2002	10010	LN4354	Sony Vaio FX-801	£1,113.54	1	£1,113.54
Black, George	18/08/2002	10010	LN3942	HP DeskJet D-155xi	£650.78	7	£4,555.46
Black, George	18/08/2002	10010	LN1376	1 Port Print Server	£76.38	1	£76.38

Figure 7.2 Microsoft Access: query results

Now we have all the information necessary to proceed to the report stage. Make sure you save your work as Salesbook Query.

It is perhaps worth discussing at this point other options available in the Query construction window. As well as selection of both field and table, you also have the option to sort the field data either in ascending or descending order. The Show tickbox is interesting as it determines whether or not that column is included in the final generated query table. This is useful if you are testing out part of a query but do not want this to be part of the final solution.

The Query construction also allows you to set a criterion for each field in question. This may be a simple criterion; for example, if you are only interested in the results of a field which are greater than seven then you set the criterion to '> 7'. It could also be a more complex criterion such as between two dates, etc.

Section 2
Constructing reports

Creating a report in many ways is similar to creating a form. First select Reports as an object in the main Access user interface. This should show two available options, namely

- Create Report in Design View;
- Create Report by using Wizard.

Select the option to 'Create Report by using Wizard'. This time, instead of using fields from tables, select the Query we created earlier, name Salesbook Query. As the Query only contains those table fields and calculated fields that we are going to use in the Report, select all the available fields using the '>>' button and select the Next button. In the next selection, choose to view the data by Customer and again select the Next button.

In the next section, the Report wizard allows you to add grouping levels. Again accept the default and select the Next button. In the next section the wizard allows sorting to take place. Accept the default for the present and step onto the next section. You are now asked about report layout – again accept the default and step on. Next you will be asked for a report style. Check out the available styles and select the one which pleases you best or accept the default style 'Corporate'.

In the last section you will be asked for a report Name. Simply call it 'Report by Customer'. You then have the option to preview the report or go to the edit mode for further modifications: select preview. Although the wizard has done a remarkable job of laying out the report there will likely be small problems associated with field labels and field sizes that it may need some manual intervention to resolve. To do this simply go back into design view and make the necessary changes (see Figure 7.3):

When complete, switch back into Print preview to make sure no further changes are necessary. This is likely to be an iterative process until you are happy with the final design. As you will notice, many of the field labels are longer than they need be and not necessarily the most descriptive in the context of a report. For example, 'NumUnits' can be better displayed as 'Qty', InvDate simply as Date, etc. This of course helps tidy the layout until you arrive at an optimum solution as in Figure 7.4.

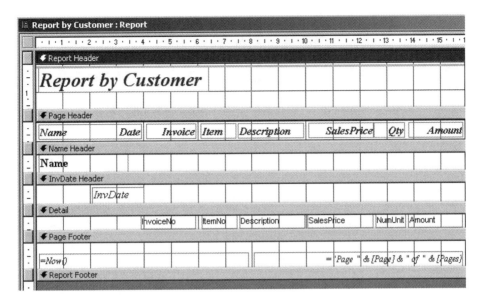

Figure 7.3 Microsoft Access: design view

Report by Customer

Name	Date	Invoice	Item	Description	SalesPrice	Qty	Amount
Black, George							
	11/08/2002						
		10003	LN3942	HP DeskJet D-155	£650.78	1	£650.78
		10003	LN1378	3 Port Print Server	£98.53	1	£98.53
	18/08/2002						
		10010	LN1376	1 Port Print Server	£76.38	1	£76.38
		10010	LN4354	Sony Vaio FX-801	£1,113.54	1	£1,113.54
		10010	LN3942	HP DeskJet D-155	£650.78	7	£4,555.46
Bruce, Mary							
	12/08/2002						
		10004	LN1173	20 m UTP Cat 5e	£5.13	50	£256.50
		10004	LN1170	10 m UTP Cat 5e	£2.86	100	£286.00
	17/08/2002						
		10009	LN4139	HP DeskJet 5550c	£178.72	4	£714.88
Evans, Charles							
	14/08/2002						
		10006	LN4354	Sony Vaio FX-801	£1,113.54	1	£1,113.54
		10006	LN4353	Sony Vaio FX-805	£1,720.20	1	£1,720.20

Figure 7.4 Microsoft Access: final report

Section 3

Role of the database administrator

After a 'hands-on' tutorial, it is worth giving some thought to the role of the database administrator (DBA).

A DBA must be a trusted employee of the company – after all they have full access to a great deal of sensitive information. Their job involves all activities related to an effectively managed database environment. Although they generally carry out the design and implementation of new systems, the majority of their work will usually centre around the management, maintenance and security of existing running systems. They also have a role in monitoring performance and ensuring that database systems run as efficiently as possible.

DBAs tend to work alone or in conjunction with the network or systems administrator. With so much of the data traffic likely to be flowing over local and wide area networks, a knowledge of networking as well as operating systems security would be a positive advantage.

The DBA must also take full authority for back-up strategies and well as instituting recovery procedures.

Quick test

1. Briefly describe the differences between the role of systems administrator and database administrator.
2. Can these be done by the same person?

Section 4

Summary

Being able to use and manipulate databases is an important key skill in today's environment. It is also a skill keenly sought after by employers. Databases appear in every industry and every facet of business. Being able to design efficient systems from real-world environments through the various stages of modelling to a production database is not only impressive but a major asset on any CV.

Section 5

Further reading

Connolly, Thomas and Carolyn Begg (2002) *Database Systems*, 3rd edn. Harlow: Addison-Wesley/Pearson Education, Chapter 9.

Chapter 8
Database security and concurrency

Chapter summary

In this chapter we are going to look at database security. We will consider the legal implications of storing certain types of data in databases as well as how this data must be protected. We will then go on to look at other aspects of both security and data integrity and in particular understand issues relating to database concurrency.

Learning outcomes

After studying this chapter, you should check your knowledge against the outcomes below and test your achievement by answering the questions at the end of the chapter. You should be able to:

Outcome 1: Understand how the Data Protection Act affects you.
You should understand the need for the Data Protection Act, what data is covered by the Act as well as who is accountable for what under the Act. You should also understand the implications the Act has for database design and use.

Outcome 2: Understand how database security and integrity are managed.
You should understand what can go wrong with a database system and the various measures that need to be enacted to ensure overall security and integrity.

How will you be assessed on this?

The Data Protection Act is an important piece of legislation which has to be understood by both user and designer alike. Depending on the course you are undertaking you may be assessed by questions relating to the eight key principles or asked to submit an essay involving both research on the Act as well as critical analysis of the eight key principles. Questions on security and data integrity are also very popular in exams, reopening earlier issues such as data integrity and data validation. The whole principle of concurrency control and deadlock are also popular exam topics.

Section 1

The Data Protection Acts of 1984 and 1998

Companies and organisations have been collecting data on individuals probably for centuries. There is nothing new about this. However, with the introduction of personal computers this situation started to change. Previously much of the data held in various paper-based systems in different companies was relatively easy to protect. Each company would look after its own collected data. Suddenly, with computers becoming networked, not only was it easier to access much of the data, it was also much easier to steal the data and leave little trace of a crime.

There was also the situation where personal data could easily become a saleable commodity to some third parties able to store, collate and use the data in ways that were never intended. This caused much concern with civil libertarians anxious to protect the rights of the individual. Indeed, around this time there were a few headline cases where individuals had loans refused, lost their jobs, etc., simply through storage of personal data that in fact proved to be incorrect. But how could an individual fight or guard against situations where companies were accessing data that may not have been fully correct and that the subject of that data had no access to?

The answer came in the form of legislation stemming from the need for Britain to comply with European guidelines such as the Convention for the Protection of Individuals with regard to Automatic Processing of Personal Data. Indeed the British government at the time feared they might lose out on trade between the UK and the other member states if such legislation was not put into force. The original legislation appeared as the Data Protection Act in 1984 covering primarily automated records but was later superseded by the Data Protection Act in 1998 to open this up to include both automated and manual records.

The Act lays out eight data protection principles:

1. Personal data must be processed 'fairly and lawfully'.

2. Personal data can only be obtained for 'specified and lawful' purposes and cannot be further processed for other purposes.

3. Personal data must be 'adequate, relevant and not excessive' in relation to the intended purpose.

4. Personal data must be 'accurate and where necessary, kept up to date'.

5. Personal data 'shall not be kept for longer than is necessary for that purpose'.

6. Personal data 'shall be processed in accordance with the rights of data subjects'.

7. Personal data must be kept secure. The Act lists measures which must be taken against 'unauthorised or unlawful processing' as well as accidental loss, destruction or damage.

8. Personal data must not be transferred to any country outside of the European Economic Area unless that country 'ensures an adequate level of protection' defined in the Act.

Any organisation that stores personal data should register with the Office of the Data Protection Registrar.

The Act provides its own interpretation of these eight principles and it is useful to make some comment on these.

1. Here the Act stresses the importance of how the data was obtained and whether the individual was 'deceived or misled' in the process.

    It is worth pointing out here that so-called 'junk mail' is not illegal provided companies are registered for this purpose. Most websites, for example, will inform you that you are being added to their mailing list and give you the opportunity to remove yourself from that list at a later stage. What you will likely also be asked is whether the company has your permission to share your information with other third-party companies. If you say 'no' then companies are not allowed to pass your information to others and could face the penalties under the Act if they fail to restrict your data.

2. If you give your permission to use your data in one context, the organisation processing the data has no right to use this data in another context. It is important that a company disclose adequately the purpose for which they are processing personal data.

3. Here the issue primarily relates to adequacy of information. An extreme example would be asking for medical data of your partner when negotiating a bank loan. If the information is not required for the immediate purpose then it gives rise to opportunity to use the data in another context which would in fact be illegal.

4. With any data collection system there has to be a means of correcting the data in the event of mistakes occurring or situations changing. Reasonable attempts must be made to ensure data is accurate. Elsewhere the Act makes provision for individuals to be given access to their data. This is one means of ensuring data is kept up to date.

5. Regular purging of processed data should be carried out. The term 'no longer than is necessary' does not necessarily relate to the processing of the data but may in fact relate to something entirely different such as an audit requirement. Either way, at some stage the data should be purged.

6. The rights of data subjects are an important feature of the Act. These include among other aspects the right to obtain copies of the information being held about them.

7. Organisations holding the data must take all necessary measures to protect the data being held. It covers such aspects as technical security (as in the use of passwords, encryption, etc.) as well as organisational security measures such as the reliability of staff that have access to the data. The Act envisages levels of security in that the measures to be taken should be in accordance with the harm that would result should such information be compromised.

8. The Act does not provide a definition of what 'appropriate security might mean'. Currently the US Department of Commerce is using their 'Safe Harbor' self-certification scheme as a means of providing evidence of compliance to the EEC directives.

Accountability under the Data Protection Act

Under the terms of the Act, the Information Commissioner reports directly to the UK Parliament. The Information Commissioner is 'a UK independent supervisory authority' whose job is to oversee and enforce both the Data Protection Act 1998 as well as the Freedom of Information Act 2000.

Within every company or organisation structure required to register under the Act, two further positions are defined, namely that of the 'data controller' as well as a 'data processor'. The terms can apply to either individuals or groups of individuals appointed by the company. The data controller is legally responsible for taking decisions on what data gets recorded within a company. A data processor, on the other hand, is an individual other than an employee who processes the data on behalf of the data controller. The Act requires that legal contracts exist between both data controller and data processor on what processing is to be carried out.

The result is a framework of accountability in the event of any problems arising as well as a high degree of transparency and openness on the purpose to which personal data is being used.

Categories of exemption to the Act

Although the Act was designed to be all embracing, there are still many categories that are specifically exempt from the Act. These include the following:

- records associated with national security;
- records associated with crime and taxation;
- records associated with health, education and social work;
- records associated with regulatory activity;
- records associated with journalism, literature and art;
- records associated with research, history and statistics;
- records associated with public information;
- records associated with disclosures required by law;
- records associated with purely domestic purposes.

Implications of the Data Protection Act for database design

The scope of the Data Protection Act relates to personal data – that is, data relating to a living individual who can be identified either directly or through some other piece of information. Whenever 'sensitive data' is involved, additional conditions are imposed. Sensitive data is defined as data relating to:

- racial or ethnic origin;
- political opinion;
- religious beliefs;
- trade union membership;
- physical or mental health;
- sexual life;
- criminal record.

In terms of database designs, the only question that need be addressed is whether the database will hold personal information on real people in a form that can identify individuals. If this is not true, then no further action need be considered. If it does contain such information then there is a clear directive to the end user to be registered under the Act.

In terms of security measures to be adopted, these fall into two main categories:

- prevention of deliberate or inadvertent access by unauthorised personnel;
- prevention of deliberate or inadvertent damage to data.

There are typically two ways of restricting access to a database. The first involves use of passwords or other forms of authentication. Generally passwords are the most cost-effective but can suffer from low security unless properly administered and understood by the relevant staff. Other forms of authentication do exist but tend to be expensive to implement. Examples of this are iris or fingerprint recognition.

The second way of dealing with this problem, in addition to passwords, would be the physical separation of the computer into a high security area accessible only through various forms of access control systems such as swipe cards, special door locks, etc. Certainly for the most sensitive of data it is advisable to disable network access if possible. Networks can be a weak link in a security system, allowing potential hackers to access data even from remote sites.

In all cases the policies and procedures set up within an organisation should be known to all employees who can effectively become the 'passive enforcer' of the procedures. Violation of these procedures should be made a disciplinary offence.

Most security violations are not committed by external hackers but by either current or ex-employees.

Quick test

What are the eight principles covered by the UK Data Protection Act?

Section 2

Security and data integrity

When considering security and data integrity, it is important to understand what can actually go wrong in the storage of data. Generally as designers of database management systems we are more concerned with setting up general data models and the overall scheme of working. As users we are more concerned about the accuracy of our own data. In other words, when we pay our credit card statement on time following receipt of a monthly statement, it is comforting to see the amount credited to your account in the following monthly statement. Unfortunately not everything runs smoothly all of the time.

We have all heard the horror stories of individuals receiving domestic gas and electricity bills in excess of £30,000. Many of the Sunday tabloids for a while made this a regular feature to highlight the stupidity of many companies' working practices. Databases generally do provide much of the basic defensive programming techniques to ensure that correct and meaningful data is entered into the system. Data entry routines can check not only data types and formats but also set limits above which special routines would have to be invoked to enter data.

But what else can go wrong?

- **Hardware failure.** From a simple power interruption through to a full hard disk 'crash', hardware is not perfect. Even any data that survives may be inconsistent and not necessarily usable.
- **Software errors.** Programmes may be running for months or even longer and still fail to show software bugs potentially hazardous to the data. Think back to the 'Millennium bug'.
- **User errors.** It is very easy, for example, for users to reverse two digits in data entry routines, thus effectively entering erroneous information.
- **Concurrency errors.** When a multi-user database is accessed simultaneously by more than one user, data used by one user may be in the process of being modified by another.
- **Deliberate damage.** This means malicious data loss or alteration by non-authorised, or even authorised, users. It could arise for example, from a virus attack.
- **Data theft.** This is not so much a problem that arises from the state of the resulting data but from the use of such unauthorised data.

Collectively, these actions can leave a database in one of two states:

- a consistent state where we may not have cause for concern;
- an inconsistent state where we immediately know some remedial action is necessary.

Consistency is the easiest matter to ascertain with regard to a database. The DBMS has the duty to maintain:

- **Entity integrity.** This is a check to ensure that, for each entity within the database, the primary key is not only unique but also non-null.
- **Referential integrity.** This is a check on the relationships between entities to ensure that there is no inconsistency. For example, all foreign keys in one table must be matched with a primary key in another table.
- **Business integrity.** This is a situation where a stored value is restrained either by some other stored data or as a result of some computation performed.

As these are fundamental to the correct working of a relational database system, any inconsistency would be immediately flagged up by the DBMS.

For data 'correctness', however, we have to rely on other tools and forms of security.

Database systems are essentially transaction-based systems. Transactions are a series of actions to be carried out by the DBMS in response to any valid request. A transaction is considered to be a logical unit of work taking a database from one consistent state to another. A transaction has two possible outcomes. It is said to be committed if the transaction completes successfully. If it is not successful, then the transaction must be aborted and return the database to the state it was in immediately before the request was made. In order to achieve this, the transaction must be 'rolled back' or 'undone'.

Transaction processes must obey the so-called 'ACID' set as defined by Haerder and Reuter (1983). This was defined as:

Atomicity	The transaction unit that must be either performed in entirety or not performed at all.
Consistency	Must take the database from one consistent state to another consistent state.
Isolation	Transactions are isolated from each other. Failure of one transaction must not affect the success of another.
Durability	A completed transaction (committed) must be permanently stored in the database and must not be lost during a subsequent transaction failure.

CIA security model approach

Database security is about taking steps to protect information contained within a database from either accidental or purposeful data access.

───────────────── CRUCIAL CONCEPT ─────────────────

It should be appreciated that being able to read certain confidential information can be just as damaging to a company as loss of the information. Computer theft does not always imply the loss of something physical as is the case with normal 'theft'.

Despite its apparent link to the American Criminal Intelligence Agency, the acronym CIA here actually stands for Confidentiality, Integrity and Availability, representing three factors on which security is often based. This approach was based on a study carried out by the Systems Security Study Committee (SSSC) back in 1991. Although the CIA model refers to overall computer security, there is clearly a strong link with security as applied to databases.

Confidentiality relates to the need to keep sensitive information private. For example, imagine the ensuing effect if an insurance company had access to an individual's health record or a company had access to another company's bid immediately before submitting their tender for a project.

Integrity here relates to ensuring that data is altered and amended by authorised means only. Think what would happen if unauthorised access could be made to your bank account or indeed academic record.

Availability relates to how available information can be made to authorised users even in the event of natural disasters, etc.

Backup and recovery

In the case of any major disaster such as a hard disk failure or total destruction of the database, backups are the prime method for recovering lost data. Periodic storage of the database to a known safe location freezes the data at a point in time. Use of tools such as transaction logs provides a way of at least knowing what data was added (and in what order) since the last backup.

The frequency of backup is important but will depend on factors such as:

- how busy the DBMS system is;
- whether there are natural periods of inactivity where backups do not cause a problem;
- the length of time it takes to make a backup.

There is a saying that the backup interval should be equal to the amount of data you are prepared to lose. In other words, if something goes wrong between backups, then all data entered since the last backup will be lost and require manual re-entry. RAID devices, which essentially keep an active mirror copy of a hard disk at all times, can help but this is no substitute for backups. RAID stands for Redundant Array of Inexpensive Disks and comes in a variety of specifications (RAID 0, RAID 2, RAID 5, etc.), each providing varying levels of protection through fault-tolerant storage devices.

CRUCIAL TIP

It is also advisable for critical databases to run the systems from an uninterrupted power supply (UPS) to ensure that the system can safely operate for a period even in the event of a total power failure.

Data validation

In order to prevent inappropriate data from corrupting and compromising a database, it is important we try to trap this type of data at an early stage. Various techniques for achieving this are possible all of which come under the general term of **data validation**.

The first thing we need to look at concerns type checking. Access allows for the provision of different data types (see the discussion in Chapter 6). Checking the entered data against the expected type of data can help in the process of screening out unwanted information. For example, if the database expects a long integer, then entering the text 'buffalo' will throw up an error.

Access also allows for the possibility of using format strings to aid data entry. For example, characters can be fielded to look like telephone numbers, postcodes or any other standard type of layout. Entries can also be verified using range checks to ensure that data entered does not fall outside of acceptable limits.

Another common technique to aid data entry is in the use of combo boxes or combinations of radio and option buttons. This greatly aids situations by only giving those sets of choices applicable to the particular situation. No longer is spelling an issue as the user simply makes a selection rather than typing in the required data.

Concurrency control

A big issue, particularly when it comes to simultaneous use by several users, is that of concurrency.

─── CRUCIAL CONCEPT ───

Concurrency control describes the process of managing simultaneous operations on a database so that they do not interfere with each other.

So why would simultaneous operations interfere with each other? Let us consider an example.

You visit a bank to withdraw some money. The teller checks your balance and finds your account has just over £80 in credit. He looks at the request for money and sees you are trying to withdraw £60. You strike up a conversation, distracting the teller from completing the transaction.

In the meantime, another bank is processing a cheque you wrote last week for £50 for a new jacket. The bank checks your account, finds you have £80 in credit and posts the transaction leaving a balance of £30.

After an extended conversation, the original bank teller realises he did not complete his transaction. He immediately posts the transaction which now records your balance as £20 in credit.

Clearly banks will not stay in business very long if they adopted this form of trading. You had £80 in your account, you withdrew £60 and paid for a £50 jacket and still have a positive balance of £20. So what went wrong?

The problem here is lack of concurrency control. Two operations were allowed to proceed concurrently in a manner that resulted in one operation interfering with the other.

Implementation of concurrency control

Most systems break down into two views on concurrency – the first termed optimistic and the second termed pessimistic. The pessimistic approach is to prevent any processing from taking place while there is the possibility of conflict. The optimistic approach is to allow all processing to proceed but to check when finished whether any conflict has arisen. If it has, then the original process must be rolled back to prevent data loss.

The choice between optimistic and pessimistic depends very much on the amount of transactions that will interfere with each other. If this is low, then an optimistic approach would make sense, accepting that if there is a problem then we can safely roll back the interfering data. On the other hand, if the number of transactions that interfere with each other is high, then switching to a pessimistic approach would likely result in a faster throughput of transactions.

If we consider first the pessimistic approach, this is generally implemented using a two-phase system of record locks. The sequence of events would largely adhere to the following pattern:

- Transactions requiring database read or write access need to utilise a system of read and write record locks.
- The DBMS will grant the locking requests provided no other transaction has a record lock associated with that particular data item.

- If a write lock exists on a particular data item, no further read or write lock will be granted until the first write lock has been removed.
- When the request for a write lock to be removed is made (with the transaction either completing or rolling back), the resulting data is made available to all (before the next write lock is applied).

With the optimistic approach, there is a slightly different pattern of events. Generally locks are not used and the system proceeds in the following manner:

- The transaction reads data as required and stores this in local memory.
- When the transaction is complete, the system checks to see that no system integrity violation has occurred. For a read operation, this should simply involve checking that the local copy of a variable is still the same as the original data. For a write operation, this would involve checking whether the output of the transaction would leave the data in a consistent state. If the answer to both is yes, then the transaction is allowed to complete, otherwise the transaction is aborted and started again.
- The database then 'commits' and writes all local storage into the main database.

Deadlock or deadly embrace

Introducing multiple locks into a system can produce its own problems. Consider the following:

System A has to process an item of data so applies a lock to the data to prevent anyone else from interfering with the data while it finishes its transaction. In the meantime System B independently locks another item of data in preparation for carrying out its own transaction.

System A also requires a second item of data but finds it locked (currently in use by System B) and so must wait to gain access. System B, on the other hand realises it also requires a second piece of data and, yes, it is also locked, this time in use by System A. System B also has to wait, and wait . . .

What we actually have here is a circular wait condition, in this case involving two parties (although technically it could involve many more parties). This situation is termed **deadlock** or **deadly embrace**.

There are several ways of dealing with deadlock but these generally fall into two camps, either prevention or detection. In the case of prevention, a system could apply all required locks at the same time rather than apply these sequentially. This would mean that one of the processes would get all required locks in place and the other would have to wait until later. In the case of detection, it is possible to monitor the lock requests to determine whether a circular wait situation was in process. If this was detected, then one of the transactions could be rolled back freeing the other to proceed.

Quick test

1. Describe what is often referred to as the CIA model of security.

2. What do we mean by concurrency control?

Section 3

Summary

Database security and integrity is an intrinsic part of modern-day database management. With the right to hold data comes the responsibility to ensure that not only must the data be accurate, but that it be used in a way that is lawful. The rights of groups and individuals can be adversely affected not only by the holding of inaccurate information but also by the use of information outside that purpose for which it was collected. It is just as important to be aware of the legal consequences of holding data as it is to correctly manipulate and handle data accurately.

Section 4

End of chapter assessment

Questions

1. What are the eight key principles embodied in the UK Data Protection Act of 1998.

2. How does the Data Protection Act classify personal data held on individuals in the following situations?
   a) Wages data held at your place of work.
   b) Medical records held in a hospital of which you are a patient.
   c) Examination results held at the university where you are a student.
   d) Political views, ethnic origin, social contacts, religious beliefs, criminal records held by the security services such as MI5.

3. What is concurrency control and why is it necessary in DBMS?

4. What is meant by deadlock and how can this be avoided?

Answers

1. The eight key principles embodied in the UK Data Protection Act of 1998 are as follows:
   a) Personal data must be processed 'fairly and lawfully'.
   b) Personal data can only be obtained for 'specified and lawful' purposes and cannot be further processed for other purposes.
   c) Personal data must be 'adequate, relevant and not excessive' in relation to the intended purpose.
   d) Personal data must be 'accurate and where necessary, kept up to date'.
   e) Personal data 'shall not be kept for longer than is necessary for that purpose'.
   f) Personal data 'shall be processed in accordance with the rights of data subjects'.
   g) Personal data must be kept secure. The Act lists measures which must be taken against 'unauthorised or unlawful processing' as well as accidental loss, destruction or damage.
   h) Personal data must not be transferred to any country outside of the European Economic Area unless that country 'ensures an adequate level of protection' defined in the Act.

2. a) Wages data is specifically excluded from the Data Protection Act provided it was obtained lawfully. As we are discussing your place of work, the inference would be that this would be lawful.

   b) Again, medical records are excluded from the Data Protection Act provided these are obtained lawfully.

   c) Examination results come into the same category as medical records and therefore also excluded for the same reasons.

   d) Here we have all the apparent problem areas which infringe the Act – but as this is related (one presumes) to national security with the involvement of MI5, then the presumption would be that this again would be excluded from the Act.

3. Concurrency control is the effective management of simultaneous operations or transactions on a database so that they do not interfere with each other. The danger with multiple-user access to a database is that operations start to interfere with each other such as the overwriting of data by one user when it is still in use by another user. This results in database inconsistencies. Concurrency control is a process to manage simultaneous access to prevent such a situation arising.

4. Deadlock is the process where a circular wait has arisen due to the implementation of concurrency control. For example, one process may lock a record and request access to another. In the meantime the requested record has been locked by another process which happens to now require access to the first record. Both processes are therefore waiting on each other to unlock the records they both control. Unless there is a procedure to release either or both records, both processes will wait indefinitely. This is called deadlock or deadly embrace.

Section 5

Further reading

Council for Europe (1981) *Convention for the Protection of Individuals with regard to Automatic Processing of Personal Data*. Strasbourg, available at http://conventions.coe.int/Treaty/en/Treaties/Html/108.htm, accessed December 2002.

Data Protection Act 1998 (1998) Stationary Office; online version available at http://www.hmso.gov.uk/acts/acts1998/19980029.htm, accessed December 2002.

Haerder, Theo and Andreas Reuter (1983) 'Principles of Transaction-Oriented Database Recovery', *Computing Surveys*, vol 15, no. 4, December.

System Security Study Committee (1990) *Computers at Risk: Safe Computing in the Information Age*. National Research Council, available at http://books.nap.edu/books/0309043883/html, pp. 49–73, accessed December 2002.

US Department of Commerce (2000) *Safe Harbor – Welcome to the Safe Harbor*, available at http://www.export.gov/safeharbor/, accessed December 2002.

Chapter 9
Introduction to SQL and DBMS access

Chapter summary

So far we have looked at communicating with Microsoft Access using its own user interface. Later in Chapter 10 we will look at a programmatic interface using connection objects such as DAO, ADO, etc. In this chapter, however, we are going to look at a third means of communicating with a DBMS, namely through Structured Query Language (SQL).

Learning outcomes

After studying this chapter, you should check your knowledge against the outcomes below and test your achievement by answering the questions at the end of the chapter. You should be able to:

Outcome 1: Understand the fundamentals of the SQL language.
You should understand some of the more important SQL syntax and constructs within the language. You should appreciate how SQL acts as both a data definition language (DDL) as well as a data manipulation language (DML).

Outcome 2: Appreciate the differences between Access SQL and Oracle SQL.
Both Oracle and Access are used widely in industry. You should be able to understand the differences between the two forms of the language.

How will you be assessed on this?

SQL tests often look not only at correct syntax but also incorrect syntax which you will be required to correct. Later in Chapter 12 you will get an opportunity to hone your skills on real problems. In this section we concentrate mainly on syntax.

Section 1

SQL basics

Structured Query language (SQL) is designed to be largely cross-platform and uses plain text as its means of communication. SQL is supported in all major relational database systems. However, it is also fair to say that there are many different 'dialects' of SQL making direct comparison between systems sometimes a little tenuous.

Structured Query Language was originally proposed by IBM back in 1974 following on from much of the work started by E. F. Codd. The prototype work was carried out on a system called System/R. It was then called SEQUEL which gives rise to much of the confusion as to whether it should be pronounced 'see-quel' or 'ess-q-ell'. Oracle was the first company to produce a commercial version of SQL in 1979 but was quickly followed by Ingres and IBM. ANSI first began to write an SQL standard in 1982 and was joined by the ISO in 1983 producing their first standard in 1987. A second version known as SQL-2 or SQL-92 was released by the ISO in 1992. Since then, various attempts have been made at SQL-3 including object-oriented constructs. Although this has appeared in several draft forms, it has never been fully accepted.

So what is SQL and what does it consist of?

SQL embodies what traditionally had consisted of three separate functional languages namely:

DDL – data definition language
DML – data manipulation language
DCL – data control language

The data definition language (DDL) is a set of instructions on how to create and destroy databases and database objects. In terms of a relational database, this comprises being able to define, for example, a table along with its various attributes, primary keys, relationships, etc. In terms of SQL, this is typically covered in the SQL CREATE instruction, for example.

The data manipulation language (DML) is a set of instructions used to query, add, delete or modify data within the database. Typical commands would include SQL SELECT, UPDATE, etc.

The data control language (DCL) is a set of instructions used to control certain aspects of the database such as security. Typical commands would include SQL GRANT and REVOKE commands, etc.

To help reinforce some of the more basic commands, we can look at some of the detailed syntax used. As we are concentrating here primarily on Access SQL we will consider commands relevant to both DDL and DML.

Note that for completeness we have included the full syntax of the SQL expression. Discussions on CONSTRAINTS are generally outside of the scope of this text.

Alter table

```
ALTER TABLE table
{ADD {COLUMN field type[(size)] [NOT NULL] [CONSTRAINT index]|
CONSTRAINT mutifieldindex}
DROP {COLUMN field|CONSTRAINT indexname}}
```

This command allows you to modify the structure of a table, such as

```
ALTER TABLE Customer ADD COLUMN Age INTEGER
```

This adds a single numeric column field Age into the Customer table.

Notice that the same command can be used to also DROP columns.

Create table

```
CREATE TABLE table (field1 type [(size)] [NOT NULL] [index1]
   [, field2 type [(size)] [NOT NULL] [index2] [, . . .]]
   [, CONSTRAINT multifieldindex [, . . .]])
```

In its most basic form this command creates a single table with a single field, for example:

CREATE TABLE Customers (Name TEXT)

This creates a table called Customers with a single text field called Name. The size of the Name field would be the default for that particular data type – in this case 50 characters.

Of course you are not restricted to only one field and you may also wish to set the size of the fields, for example:

CREATE TABLE Customers (FirstName TEXT (20),
    LastName TEXT (20))

If it is important that valid data must be entered into a field, then you should include the phrase NOT NULL after the appropriate field. If you do not enter data you will then receive a warning during data entry.

CREATE TABLE Customers (FirstName TEXT (20),
LastName TEXT (20) NOT NULL)

In addition, you may want to include some constraint on the data or combination of data – for example, if you wish all three fields being entered to be unique, then you could use the following:

CREATE TABLE Customers (FirstName TEXT (20),
    LastName TEXT (20),
    DateOfBirth DATETIME,
    CONSTRAINT MultiConstraint UNIQUE (FirstName, LastName, DateOfBirth))

You may also wish to set the primary key of the table. If this is a single key then it can be achieved thus:

CREATE TABLE Customers (FirstName TEXT (20),
    LastName TEXT (20) NOT NULL PRIMARY KEY)

In the situation where more than one field constitutes the primary key, this would be achieved thus:

CREATE TABLE Customers (FirstName TEXT (20) NOT NULL,
    LastName TEXT (20) NOT NULL,
    PRIMARY KEY (FirstName, LastName))

In a similar manner, you may also wish to express a relationship to a primary key in another table. This would be achieved as follows:

CREATE TABLE TestDrive
    (VehicleNo integer Not Null,
    CustomerNo integer Not Null references Customer(CustomerNo),
    TestDate datetime,
    DComments text(50),
    primary key (VehicleNo, CustomerNo))

Here CustomerNo field has been related to CustomerNo in the Customer Table.

Delete

DELETE [table, *] FROM table WHERE criteria

For example, to delete all records from a table, you could enter

DELETE * FROM Customer

On the other hand, if you only wished to delete records that met a specific criterion then you would use the following construct:

DELETE * FROM Customer WHERE Town = 'Newcastle'

Drop table

DROP TABLE tablename

As well as creating tables, DDL also allows you to delete tables using the DROP command. It should be said, however, that you cannot drop a table which has one of its fields declared as a foreign key in another table.

Insert into

INSERT INTO target [(field1[, field2[, . . .]])] VALUES (value1[, value2 [, . . .])

This command allows data to be inserted into a table. Examples could include

INSERT INTO Customer
VALUES ('Robert Dean', '23 Park Avenue', 'Roker', 'Sunderland')

INSERT also allows a reduced entry set by simply specifying the fields in question, such as:

INSERT INTO Customer (Name, Town)
VALUES ('Robert Dean', 'Sunderland')

Select

This is by far the most important of all the SQL commands as it forms the basis for construction of all queries.

The simplest query would be:

SELECT * from Customer

This simply selects all columns from a table called Customer listing out all records.

SELECT Firstname, Surname FROM Customer
WHERE Salary > 23000

In this case we have only selected two attributes from the table Customer and only requested those records which meet the criterion of Salary > £23,000.

The format of the SELECT command is complex and better covered in a tutorial. For this reason we will leave most of the explanation for this command until Chapter 12 where we can try out many SELECT commands and instantly see their effect.

Update

UPDATE table SET newvalue WHERE criteria

The UPDATE command is used to change data in either some or all of the records within a table. It doesn't generate a set of results so you cannot tell immediately which records were affected. To see which records are to be affected, it is advisable to run a SELECT query using the same criteria:

UPDATE staff_data
SET salary = salary * 1.05

This would globally give all staff in the staff data table a 5 per cent rise.

Of course, for one poor individual, you may wish to reduce his salary after a change of responsibilities. This could be achieved using:

```
UPDATE staff_data
SET salary = salary – 5000
WHERE empoyeeID = 12432
```

Quick test

Name the three functional languages embodied in SQL, briefly describing the function of each.

Section 2

Comparison between Oracle and Access SQL

The Oracle database system was entirely written around SQL and is still today generally regarded as the leading exponent of this method of database access. However, as previously mentioned, most major databases also provide SQL access to their database leading to reasonably close correlations of commands. As we have concentrated primarily on the Microsoft Access database system in this book, it is worth drawing together the main differences between Microsoft Access SQL and Oracle SQL.

Oracle's main user interface for SQL commands is SQL*Plus. The SQL*Plus interface is text based but provides limited editor-style facilities. Lines terminated with a semicolon are treated as immediate commands executing both current and any previous lines. Lines not terminated with a semicolon are treated as lines in an editor and do not execute when entered. This enables the build up of fairly complex queries. There are also limited editor commands such as append, change string, etc. Although all necessary operations can be achieved using the SQL*Plus interface, we have found that most students still prefer to use a separate editor and 'cut and paste' the query into the SQL*Plus interface window for subsequent execution. Once tested and proved, the query can be left on the editor while another is built. This makes it easier to save a student's work at the end of a session.

Microsoft Access, on the other hand, makes access to the SQL pane a little more difficult. It is accessed not as a program but through the Query object. First select 'Create query in Design View' and close down the Show table dialogue. You are then free to switch to SQL View on the menu bar. Once you gain access to the SQL query pane, it can be used in conjunction with a text editor (such as NotePad) to test out queries. It is also a text-based user interface. Again similar to the SQL*Plus use with an editor, once tested and proved, the query can be left on the editor while another is built. Again this makes it easy to save a student's work at the end of the session. Microsoft SQL View does not support the use of a semicolon for immediate operation.

Command differences

- Command differences between Microsoft Access SQL and Oracle SQL tend to be ideological rather than functional in that these conform closer to the Microsoft standard for common user interface. The first and most obvious difference is that Microsoft allows the use of spaces within table or field names. Most other SQL implementations do not support spaces. To embody spaces, Microsoft expects the use of square brackets around the field or table name, such as [Property for rent].

- In Oracle, the word 'as' is optional in an alias statement. In Access, this is not optional. For example:

  select first_name, second_name name from customer

  would be perfectly valid in Oracle but not in Access. Alternatively

  select first_name, second_name as name from customer

  would be perfectly valid for both Access and Oracle.

- Microsoft uses '&' as the concatenation operator whereas Oracle uses the double pipe '‖' to achieve the same function.

  The following statements would be functional equivalent in the two dialects:

  Select second_name & ', ' & first_name from customer

  Select second_name ‖', '‖ first_name from customer

- Oracle uses the substr function to return part of a string. Microsoft has its own string handling functions. For example, consider the following as equivalent statements:

  substr(first_name, 1, 1) is the same as left(first_name, 1)

  substr(name, 5, 4) is the same as mid(name, 5, 4)

- Oracle supports padding functions such as Rpad and Lpad which do not appear in Access. However, Access supports many other functions which could easily be used to construct such instructions.

- Oracle supports the upper and lower functions to force capitalisation or transfer to lower case. Access equivalent functions are LCase and UCase.

- Oracle uses a function called sysdate to refer to the current date of transaction. Access uses the date function.

Although many of the functions use alternative names, there are actually few major implementation differences between Oracle and Access that would prevent one implementation from being quickly transferred to the other.

Data definition language differences

As well as command differences, there is a major difference between Oracle SQL and Access SQL concerning the use of commit and rollback statements in Oracle. Basically, Oracle data does not get stored into the database until a COMMIT statement has been given. If the rollback statement is subsequently made, then the data added can simply be undone. This does not happen with Access SQL.

To be fair, Access uses a lightweight version of SQL called Microsoft JET SQL. This is not the same product as that used on their heavyweight product SQL Server 2000 and later versions. For a fairer comparison between products, Oracle should be compared to SQL Server.

Quick test

1. What is the name of the main user interface for Oracle's SQL commands?

2. Does Microsoft Access have an equivalent user interface?

Section 3

Summary

SQL is an important language with which to communicate with relational databases. These can be from different suppliers or, as we will also find out, running on different platforms. In the next chapter we will explore the whole issue of client/server databases operating within a network or on a distributed basis.

Section 4

End of chapter assessment

Questions

1. Explain the difference between a data definition language (DDL) and a data manipulation language (DML) and give an example of how SQL can achieve both.

2. Convert the following Access SQL queries to Oracle format:
   a) SELECT [Staff Name]
      FROM Staff
   b) SELECT Surname & ', ' & Forenames
      FROM Customer
   c) SELECT Surname, left(Forenames, 1)
      FROM Customer

Answers

1. A data definition language is primarily concerned with structure of the database by creation or deletion of either databases or database objects (such as tables). A data manipulation language is concerned with the querying, modifying, adding or deletion of data with that structure.

   SQL is capable of handling both sets of commands:
   – An example of a DDL command would be the CREATE instruction.
   – An example of a DML command would be the SELECT instruction.

2. a) The problem we have here is that Oracle cannot handle spaces within column names. The column name would need to be changed to be a single word such as StaffName. The resulting Oracle query could then be:

      SELECT StaffName
      From Staff

b) Oracle does not use the ampersand as a concatenation operator. Instead Oracle uses ‖. The resulting query would therefore be:

SELECT Surname ‖', '‖ Forenames
FROM Customer

c) Oracle has its own form of string handling functions called 'substr'. The resulting query would then be:

SELECT Surname, substr(Forenames, 1, 1)
FROM Customer

Section 5

Further reading

DevGuru (2002) *Microsoft JET SQL Version 3.0*, available at http://www.devguru.com, accessed November 2002.

Chapter 10
Distributed and networked databases

Chapter summary

In this chapter we are going to look at the other main interface with database systems such as Microsoft Access, namely a programmatic interface. We are going to look at the whole issue of client/server architecture and the use of databases in a network environment. Network computing has in recent years become one of the fastest growing areas within computing with most companies and institutions now wholly reliant on the operation and well-being of their networks.

Learning outcomes

After studying this chapter, you should check your knowledge against the outcomes below and test your achievement by answering the questions at the end of the chapter. You should be able to:

Outcome 1: Appreciate the three main types of network databases.
Despite the large number of databases which run in a stand-alone mode, the greatest application of databases is in a shared or networked environment. You should be able to appreciate the three main types of databases running in such an environment, namely client/server, web and distributed databases.

Outcome 2: Understand the need for a programmatic interface.
Database systems used within a networked or distributed environment require custom programs in order to function. You should be able to understand some of the technologies necessary to achieve this interface.

How will you be assessed on this?

Questions on networked and distributed databases are common in exams. A thorough knowledge of the three main models (client/server, web and distributed) is essential. On the programmatic side, it is unlikely this will feature greatly although knowledge of this area will greatly assist in later work such as project web construction. Gone are the days when web-based projects consisting solely of HTML pages will be acceptable for all but the introductory web-design modules. Generally students will be expected to provide back-end database integration to their web projects.

Section 1

Network computing

It may at first seem strange looking at network computing within a study text on databases but networked and distributed databases play such a major role in the field of DBMS systems. There are at least three main categories of database systems that run on networks of varying descriptions, namely

- client/server databases;
- web databases;
- distributed databases.

In the 1960s and 1970s, computing was carried out on mainframe systems. These were very large and exceedingly expensive systems taking them out of the reach of all but the largest companies and organisations. Database systems were around but were based on a vertical distributed model with all processing passing through the central mainframe computer (see Figure 10.1).

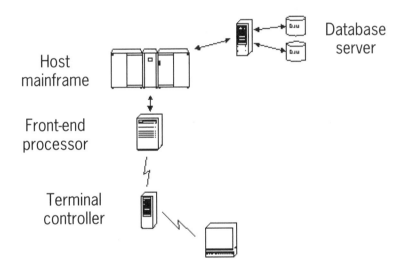

Figure 10.1 Early database system

In the 1970s, mini-computers started to appear with the personal computer arriving in the late 1970s and early 1980s. Computers started to appear on every desk within a company or organisation. This in turn led to the need to share data and information through connectivity or local area networks.

The architecture that most suited the new DBMS systems was based on the horizontal distributed architecture with client computers being able to request data over a network from a server database.

Figure 10.2 shows a typical horizontally distributed architecture. The UNIX server shown in the diagram services what could be a large number of distributed processing applications connected to the network. This is the basis of the client/server model. The horizontal network also supports distributed database applications which we will discuss later in the chapter.

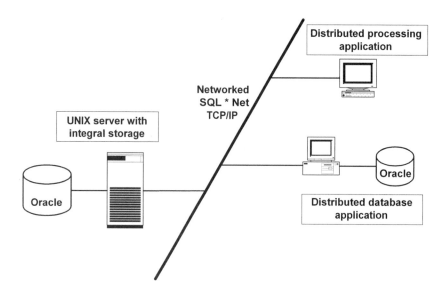

Figure 10.2 Typical horizontally distributed architecture

Although there were many network protocols and formats, TCP/IP developed by DARPA as part of the Internet protocol suite for UNIX has been largely universally adopted and is the world's most common networking protocol. As the protocol adopted for the Internet, TCP/IP has been implemented on every major computer platform allowing a high degree of interoperability between computers operating on different platforms.

Quick test

What is the main connectivity protocol used in most networked database applications?

Section 2

Client/server architecture

Having a multitude of databases containing various interrelated pieces of information can lead to severe updating problems. Versioning control helps but it is soon difficult to tell what data is the latest on which database and there is the possibility of making wrong decisions based on out-of-date information. What would be more beneficial would be a single database to which everyone has access. The client/server database is simply that.

One machine is designated the server and hosts the database. When a client machine wishes to query or update the database, it sends the information to the server which acts on its behalf. The results of the operation are then passed back to the client which made the original request. As database access is only a small part of the work of a database system, the server can service a large number of clients.

With the era of the graphical user interface (GUI such as Windows etc.), the amount of data being processed by the client machine has increased considerably over the last twenty years. However, as the server only deals with data requests, there is no reason at the server end to format the data suitable for GUI display – indeed this would be a positive disadvantage as it would result in higher network traffic and slower apparent response time of the client computer. There is therefore a 'division of labour' with the client taking care of all GUI activities and interaction with the user and the server communicating with many clients using very 'raw' or simple data.

The main advantages of the client/server approach relates to the fact that there is only one database, making such situations as transaction control, concurrency control as well as system security relatively easy to handle. Of course, the distinction between client and server can often be blurred. It is not unusual for a server to use the services of another server, effectively itself becoming the client. In fact any machine could be both a client as well as a server, the distinction being determined by the applications running rather than its hardware configuration. This is often termed a peer-to-peer relationship.

Quick test

In a client/server database system, which end creates and manipulates graphical interfaces and why?

Section 3

Web databases

In reality web databases are very similar to client/server database systems other than the fact that responses from the server must be in HTML using HTTP protocols. This typically leads to a much slower response time between the two types of system.

While client/servers traditionally consist of a two-layer model, web databases (as with many of the larger client/server systems) have generally moved over to a three-layer architecture in the interests of scalability. This is illustrated in Figure 10.3.

In this three-tier arrangement, clients are outside the control of the main system. Requests sent from the clients are handled by the web or application server which handles not only the business logic of the system but also serves web pages to the client for viewing. If required, this will also request services from the services of the database server.

Communications over the Web are mainly based on the Hypertext Transport Protocol (HTTP). In this form of communications, requests are processed and terminated as though the client had broken the communications session. This is necessary for reasons of scalability. With a large indeterminate number of connections, the server would soon be overloaded and 'crash'. While this works well for normal web page delivery, clearly it does not suit a database type application where follow-up queries may be required such as to display the next 10 rows. Unless the database knows both the query and which rows you are talking about then clearly there are problems.

Browsers use a system of 'cookies' to keep track of any persistent data they may wish to store about a previous visit to that website. These are small text files usually hidden away in the 'bowels' of the operating system where they cannot be

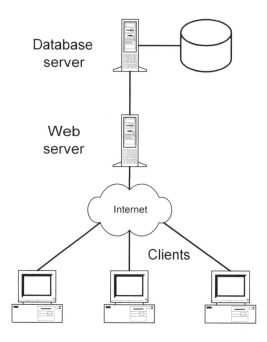

Figure 10.3 Web database three-layer architecture

accidentally erased. Erasing these files is not strictly speaking detrimental but you may find yourself having to log back in as a new user, for example. Cookies can assist in resolving repeated queries by passing back to the web server information associated with a previous state.

The integration of databases into websites is now commonplace using a variety of associated technologies. Examples of these include Common Gateway Interface (CGI), Server APIs, Active Server Pages (ASP), Personal Home Page (PHP), Javascript, Java servlets and Java Server Pages (JSP).

Quick test

Unlike their client/server counterparts, web databases do send GUI data over the network. Why is this?

Section 4

Distributed systems

Distributed systems break many rules as they in fact consist of several databases generally geographically separated, and may exist on different platforms or even use different models (e.g. relational and object oriented). Such systems exist for two reasons, the first being to look after their own clients in the event that there are no communications between server systems. An important aspect of this type of distributed system is being able to recover a joint understanding between systems when communications have been restored. This brings in many aspects related to recovery control and of course concurrency.

The second and more common understanding of distributed systems is that they serve only part of the 'marketplace'. In other words, different data would be deliberately held on different databases with a view to communal sharing. The reason for this relates to an attempt to cut down the amount of network data traffic between database systems. Although the individual systems may be connected to a high speed LAN, processing this would be many orders of magnitude slower than if the data was held in one common repository.

Let us imagine a typical scenario with a company having two sites. Assume one of the sites primarily deals with manufacturing with the other site handling all the accounts-related data. Having a single database stored at either location means the inevitable data traffic associated with the other location. What we require is some form of data separation or partitioning of the database to keep most of the traffic such that it can be handled on a local basis. Generally there are three such schemes in existence, namely:

- partitioned system;
- horizontal fragmentation;
- vertical fragmentation.

With a partitioned system, different tables would be held at the different sites. This generally works well in situations where some of the tables may be largely irrelevant to another particular location. It doesn't exclude the tables from being queried from another site but the likelihood of this happening would be small.

With horizontal fragmentation, each site would be responsible for a certain number of rows within each table determined by the key value of the table. For example, Plant A may be responsible for customers 1 to 100 with Plant B being responsible for customers 101 to 200. Only Plant A would enter data concerning its customers with Plant B entering data concerning its customers.

Vertical fragmentation refers to situations where tables are split by column with different sites having the responsibility of updating their respective columns. This could occur in a situation where part of a record is controlled by one plant (say the order processing) and the remainder of the record is controlled by another (as in an accounts department). Of course, there is one obvious problem with vertical fragmentation in that the table primary key would have to be kept at both sites in order to correctly access the various records.

Replication

While it is convenient to maintain a fragmented database at different locations to cut down network traffic and enable more responsive behaviour, at some stage you will need to query the whole database. Querying over a distributed network is generally slow. This is due not only to the network speed but is further exaggerated by the necessity to maintain concurrency etc.

Another approach to this problem is through the use of data replication. Data replication involves storing copies of the data held by the various fragments either at one master site or indeed at all sites. There are dangers with this approach mainly due to issues related to data consistency and concurrency. However, replication is effective in situations where sites may only require data access for reference only. Companies often circulate data at predetermined intervals for local reference use without expecting this to be updated by the local centre.

Transparency

One of the main design goals of any distributed system is to try and maintain a high degree of transparency in its operations. By transparency here we mean the user should not be especially aware of any differences resulting from how or indeed where the data is stored. There are essentially three areas of concern with regard to transparency. These are the location of the data, how the data is fragmented over the network and whether some form of replication is being used. Users of the system should be able to query as though the system was a single local database and not be concerned how the DBMS manages issues such as location, fragmentation or replication.

Querying distributed databases

Querying a distributed database is obviously more complex than querying a single database. The issue of transparency dictates that the problems associated with such queries must be handled in a transparent way by the DBMS. However, it is worth considering how such processes actually do take place.

Quick test

Explain the difference between horizontal and vertical fragmentation.

Section 5

Programmatic control

Until now, we have talked only about Microsoft Access running as a complete database system. However, with the new demands of client/server, web or distributed systems, clearly there is a need for a full programmatic interface. In short, there has to be a considerable amount of bespoke software written to support the overall needs of the system. We can therefore look on software such as Microsoft Access in a multi-user environment as being a database component which will require integration into a larger piece of software.

Communication between software and a database

In the 1980s, the only real portable interface for applications communicating with a relational database was the use of embedded SQL which consisted of a language-specific pre-compiler. Essentially SQL commands could be embedded into a host programming language such as COBOL and C. While this worked, it was laborious and time-consuming. What was required was an application programming interface (API) which could be used directly from the programming language.

Microsoft developed ODBC (Open Database Connectivity) to take care of this need in the early 1990s (see Figure 10.4). Later Sun developed their equivalent API called JDBC to provide the same connectivity, this time with object-oriented systems.

Essentially as a programmer all you need to do is to use the ODBC API. The API in turn communicates through a custom driver to a vendor-specific database. Using such an arrangement effectively isolates you as the programmer from the differences in communications with the database of your choice.

Microsoft have gone on to develop a whole range of data access objects used within their programming languages such as VB, VB.NET, C, C++, C#, etc. All of these

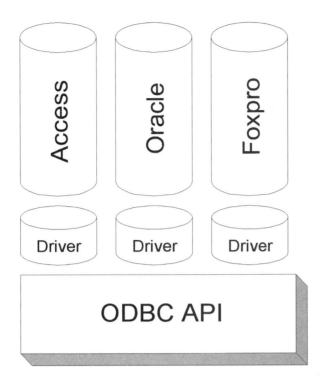

Figure 10.4 Database connectivity

objects utilise ODBC as their means of communicating with various vendor-specific databases. These data access objects include:

DAO – data access objects
RDO – remote data objects
ADO – active data objects

Of the three, Microsoft are actively promoting ADO as their preferred data model.

A typical ODBC interface with a Microsoft Access database using Visual Basic and standard security would be:

```
oConn.open "Driver={Microsoft Access Driver (*.mdb)};" &_
    "Dbq=c:\path\dbName.mdb;" &_
    "Uid=admin;" &_
    "Pwd="
```

As this book is not intended to cover software programming, we will do no more than mention the existence of such programming objects at this point.

In the case of a web interface, the interfaces remain the same, only the means of programming changes. Instead of languages such as C++ or VB, web interfaces use systems such as ASP utilising VBScript or PHP to contain the programme.

Sun also have equivalent programming such as JavaScript and Java Server Pages (JSP).

Quick test

Describe the use of ODBC or JDBC in a program-driven environment.

Section 6

Summary

Distributed and networked databases account for some of the most important mission-critical systems around. Companies are becoming more and more reliant on shared information on local area networks, on wide area networks and of course on the Internet. These systems generally require a considerable amount of programming to ensure they meet the level of performance and expectations necessary for deployment within a company situation.

Section 7

End of chapter assessment

Questions

1. Explain the concept of the client/server in the context of a database system. Is it possible for a server also to be a client?

2. Describe the types of fragmentation and partitioning used in distributed databases. What special problems are generally encountered with vertical fragmentation?

3. Web databases are client/server by nature and yet typically use a 'three-layer' architecture rather than the 'two-layer' architecture often used in a client/server database system. Explain why this is desirable.

Answers

1. Client/server is the name given to a process where one party (the client) requests database services and the other party (the server) attempts to fulfil these requests. In reality, there can be many clients all requesting the services of the one database server.

   Client/servers typically work within a network environment. Sending all user interface information to the server for processing would soon overwhelm the server with the various clients acting as 'dumb terminals'. By making the client responsible for user interface functions and graphical displays, this dramatically cuts down the amount of work required from the server. It also cuts down even more dramatically the volume of data passing backwards and forwards from client to server. This allows the server time to service a multitude of clients.

   It is common even within a client/server relationship for the server to, in turn, request certain services from another server. Within this context a server can also be termed a client.

2. Partitioning in the context of a distributed system is where we store different tables from a common system in separate locations. Horizontal fragmentation is the term used when we store data from different rows in common tables held at different sites. For example, if we assume a primary key of CompanyNo, then the

details of Companies 1 to 99 may be stored at one location whereas the details of Companies 100 to 199 may be stored at a different location. Although a table by the same name would exist at two sites, these would not be confused as only one location would process data for a particular company.

Vertical fragmentation occurs where only certain columns within a table are updated and processed at one particular site. As an example, assume that the whole row (or record) contains both manufacturing as well as sales-related data. Only the columns associated with manufacturing would then be updated at one site whereas columns associated with sales would be updated at another site.

The special problem that exists in vertical fragmentation is that the table primary key must be maintained at both sites rather than only at one site.

3. The client end of a web database is not part of the website system and as such is not available for programming. The server end must contain all of the business logic associated with the queries as well as take care of all database requests. It also has to take care of many of the user interface arrangements (in this case serve out the web pages) normally carried out by the client in a traditional client/server arrangement.

To get over this problem, a three-layer architecture is usually implemented with a web server taking care of all non-database requests.

Section 8

Further reading

Date, Chris (1987) *An Introduction to Database Systems. Vols I and II*, 4th edn. Addison-Wesley, Boston, MA, USA.

Chapter 11
More database models

Chapter summary

So far we have primarily concentrated on the relational model of data although we briefly introduced some earlier models, namely the hierarchical and the network models. In this chapter we will look at several other models including object-oriented and object-relational, as well as one interesting recent development, namely that of the XML database.

Learning outcomes

After studying this chapter, you should check your knowledge against the outcomes below and test your achievement by answering the questions at the end of the chapter. You should be able to:

Outcome 1: Understand the basis of other data models currently available.
You should be aware of some of the other main data models in use today such as object-oriented and object-relational.

Outcome 2: Examine the basis for some of the newer data models.
You should also be aware of multimedia databases as well as the new emerging XML model for data.

How will you be assessed on this?

Assessment will depend largely on the course you are following. An understanding of the different model types will be essential as well as an appreciation of the uses and the technologies behind the data models. These often will appear as an essay-style assignment question as part of your coursework.

Section 1

The object-oriented database

Object-oriented (OO) programming developed primarily through the late 1970s and 1980s initially from a language called Smalltalk but it was also adopted by languages such as C++ and much later by Java. All data is protected through a system called 'encapsulation' and can only be modified by the object's own 'methods', that is, pieces of software written to carry out specific functions. Collectively these methods describe the object's 'behaviour'. Once the behaviour of the object has been defined and proven, other objects can adopt the same behaviour through a process called 'inheritance'.

Within the OO program will be a collection of objects that communicate with each other by means of messages. For example, to start a car object, we simply send a 'start car' message to the particular car object which will in turn alter the data stored in the car object using the 'start car' method to indicate that the car is running. Such a system ensures that data associated with one object never corrupts data associated with another object.

Object-oriented databases have a major advantage over their relational counterparts in that objects can be stored literally in the structure of the object. This means that there is no need to carry out any mapping between the real-world entities and the storage within the database. Indeed, many programmers use this aspect as a means of achieving data 'persistence' within their programs. But popularity with programmers is not matched with equal popularity among end users. Relational tables are easy to understand and implement whereas objects can be complex and difficult to describe within a user interface such as Oracle or Access. For this reason object-oriented databases (OODB) do not exist as a stand-alone product with its own 'Access-style' interface.

It was always widely expected that object-oriented databases would have a major impact on the relational database. Relational databases did not fit in well with object programming due to the table structures and its lack of inheritance. Databases such as Gemstone and Iris appeared early in the process with others such as ObjectStore, O2, Versant, Objectivity and Poet appearing later in the 1980s and 1990s. However, these never achieved their expected potential. What is perhaps even more surprising is the number of OO programmers who continued to regularly use relational databases despite the obvious mismatch in programming concepts.

There are some notable exceptions where object-oriented databases are in fact highly successful. Programs such as computer-aided design (CAD) packages with their high dependence on inherited objects seem to be particularly well suited to the object-oriented database. Nevertheless, programmers bucked the anticipated trend of moving everything over to the object-oriented approach by sticking with their existing relational database approach.

Like relational databases, object-oriented databases also need a manipulation and query language in order to be used successfully within a client/server or other multi-user environment. In response, the Object Data Management Group put forward their proposed standard for an Object Definition Language as well as an Object Query Language (OQL). These were modelled on the basis of SQL and, indeed, try as far as possible to mimic many of the SQL statements.

Quick test

With so many advantages over relational databases in an object-oriented environment, why are object-oriented databases not more successful?

Section 2

The object-relational or extended-relational database

There is little doubt that there are considerable amounts of money to be made from database management systems. According to Gartner Dataquest, database

Table 11.1 Sales of database licences

Company	2001 revenue	% of market share
IBM (including Informix)	$3.06 billion	34.6
Oracle	$2.83 billion	32.0
Microsoft	$1.44 billion	16.3
Sybase	$0.234 billion	2.6
Others	$1.27 billion	14.4

Source: Gartner Dataquest.

software licence sales for the year 2001 accounted for the statistics given in Table 11.1.

With the growth in object-oriented programming, many at the time felt it was only a matter of time before the relational database would be largely superseded by the object-oriented database. This, as can be seen in the 2001 figures, did not happen. However, in the intervening years, more and more traditional relational model databases such as Oracle and Informix started to support object-oriented features. Whether through altruistic notions of product enhancement or crude attempts to strangulate at birth the possible success of a competing data model, the overall result was still the same. What was needed was the formulation of a new all-embracing model.

Now called the object-relational model, several authors have attempted to define what an object-relational database actually is. Michael Stonebraker and Dorothy Moore, in their 1996 book *Object-Relational DBMSs: The Next Great Wave*, state: 'These are relational in nature because they support SQL; they are object-oriented in nature because they support complex data.'

At least for the foreseeable future, the inclusion of object-oriented features into relational databases has been met with solid market approval.

Quick test

Are object-relational databases any more successful than object-oriented databases? Justify your answer.

Section 3

The multimedia database

There is currently a lot of research taking place into multimedia database systems. Such systems are capable of carrying out pattern match searches within images and sounds as well as encompassing the whole field of electronic document management.

Many relational database management systems support to a limited extent the storage of certain multimedia files within a database environment. In Chapter 6, for example, we saw that Access supports OLE (object linking and embedding) objects as a specific data type. This allows for storage of up to 1 GB of object such as a bitmap, sound, video, etc. However, storage is not the only matter to be considered with regard to a multimedia database. New methods of data searching, comparison and extrapolation are necessary to achieve useful results.

Specific examples of multimedia databases are available on the Internet but a simpler example would be a product such as Microsoft Encarta where the database integrates pictures, sounds and text in a variety of formats and integrates these spatially within a browser type of environment.

Quick test

What is the main characteristic of a multimedia database?

Section 4

The XML database

With the explosion of Internet services over the last few years and the promise of much greater awareness and use of electronic commerce, the need for database integration is part and parcel of modern-day website design. Whether you are searching for a book at your favourite web bookstore or paging through your statements at your internet banking account, databases are required to furnish data in the form of HTML pages.

HTML was originally developed as a subset of SGML for use on the World Wide Web. SGML or Standard Generalized Markup Language was developed by Charles F. Goldfab and adopted by the ISO in 1986. SGML is in fact a standard for the description of markup languages and is in effect a meta language, i.e. a language about a language. A markup language must specify essentially three things:

- What markup is allowed and what is required.
- How the markup is distinguished from the actual text.
- What the markup specifically means.

HTML was originally conceived in a text-based environment only later becoming graphical. The markup originally conceived was very simple dealing essentially with layout and presentation. While this works well for humans reading screen information, it does not facilitate the situation where data is required by systems for subsequent processing. For example, suppose we need to send a formula such as:

$$v_x = \int_0^t a_x$$

This may in itself not appear to be so complex but with HTML, the only option available is to take a picture of the formula and store this as a graphics file (GIF for example). Although this will be completely readable to humans, it cannot be transferred directly to another program still retaining its meaning. It is, after all, only a bitmap image.

For effective electronic commerce we need to be able to pass information over the web that is interoperable by nature, i.e. it must be able to be read by any computer platform (PC, MAC, IBM, etc.) running any operating system (Windows, UNIX, etc.). ASCII text is still the best hope for interoperability between systems and text-based markup languages hold the key.

In order to facilitate the development of markup languages for the Web, XML was developed simplifying much of the original SGML specification but also opening it up for use in multi-language, multi-character set environments. Indeed, with XML you are allowed to generate any tag you may wish (within certain restrictions) to provide the necessary markup for an application. For example in the case of the above formula, this can be represented in MathML as:

```
<?xml version="1.0" encoding="UTF-8"?>
<math display="block" xmlns="http://www.w3.org/1998/Math/MathML">
  <msub>
    <mrow>
      <mi>v</mi>
    </mrow>
    <mrow>
      <mi>x</mi>
    </mrow>
  </msub>
  <mo>=</mo>
  <munderover>
    <mrow>
      <mo>&int;</mo>
      <msub>
        <mrow>
          <mi>a</mi>
        </mrow>
        <mrow>
          <mi>x</mi>
        </mrow>
      </msub>
    </mrow>
    <mrow>
      <mn>0</mn>
    </mrow>
    <mrow>
      <mi>t</mi>
    </mrow>
  </munderover>
</math>
```

While on the surface this may appear as a long-winded attempt at a simple formula, any computer capable of reading ASCII and understanding MathML can not only display the formula but could potentially use it.

XML databases

The XML is based on a tree-like structure and does not fit comfortably with either the table-like structure of the relational database system or indeed the object-like structure of the object-oriented database system. Developers are currently using their own mapping methods mainly to relational databases much like the early days of object-oriented programming.

Native XML databases are starting to appear on the market such as Tamino XML Server, Xyleme Zone Server, ozone, Lore, Impedo XML Database, eXtensible Information Server, etc.

What is also interesting, however, is the number of existing database systems that claim to be XML enabled. These currently include:

- rational/object relational:
  - IBM DB2
  - IBM Informix
  - Microsoft Access 2002
  - Microsoft FoxPro
  - Microsoft SQL Server 2002
  - Oracle 8i and 9i
  - Sybase ASE12.5
- Object oriented:
  - Objectivity/DB
  - Versant enJin.

Whether this is a genuine attempt to enhance the product line or simply a divisive means to maintain market share only time will tell. For the moment there is a great deal of interest in XML as the next major database model.

Quick test

Why is XML such an important concept?

Section 5

Other data models

We stressed in an earlier chapter that much of the success of the relational data model is associated with the mathematical underpinning it received from set theory and its associated relational algebra. It is therefore worth mentioning two other areas where a great deal of mathematical activity is currently taking place.

Tree (or hedge) automata

Tree (or hedge) automata and tree languages started back in the 1960s with Buchi and Wright. They used tree languages in the representation of hierarchically organised structures. More recently Mokoto Murata proposed the use of hedge automata as a formal model for XML schema.

Higher order logic

Category theory has been around since 1945 appearing in Eilenberg and Mac Lane's paper 'General Theory of Natural Equivalences'. In the late 1950s and 1960s, category theory developed quickly, mainly in the context of algebraic geometry, algebraic topology and universal algebra.

Category theory has long been considered a 'foundational' alternative to set theory but has yet to prove itself in that context. It certainly has all the hallmarks of being as significant to database theory as did set theory back in the 1960s and 1970s.

Current work going on in this field includes that of Mike Heather (Newcastle University), Nick Rossiter (Northumbria University) and David Nelson (Sunderland University).

Quick test

Explain the term Higher Order Logic and its relationship to set theory.

Section 6

Summary

In this chapter we have looked at many of the other data models vying for success within a global market economy. Some will no doubt die. Others will be incorporated into existing models. Most, however, will find their own niche market and play their part in the grand order of databases.

Section 7

End of chapter assessment

Questions

1. Critically examine the role played by the major relational database companies such as IBM, Oracle and Microsoft in migrating their products over to be object relational. Critically examine the need for such a change at that time. Are we likely to see an XML object-relational database with multimedia extensions in due time?

2. Database management systems such as SQL Server, Informix and Oracle have all started to include XML interfaces into their products. Examine the need for such interfaces and give an assessment on whether you believe the XML Data model is critical to the success of business-to-business (B2B) e-commerce.

3. Critically examine the role of the multimedia data model and give your views on whether such a data model is likely to have major impact or exist in a niche market.

Answers

We have deliberately left out the answers to this section as these would only be an opinion which would be neither right nor wrong. In all critical assessments of this type it is more important to show you have done your research, examined the arguments from various sides and put forward your opinion with reasons for adopting what may in fact be a controversial viewpoint.

Section 8

Further reading

Bourret, R. P. (2002) *XML and Databases*, available at www.rpbourret.com/xml/ XMLAndDatabases.htm, accessed December 2002.

Cattell, R. G. G. and Douglas Barry et al. (2000) *The Object Data Standard: ODMG 3.0*. Morgan Kaufmann Publishers, San Francisco, CA, USA.

Date, C. J. and Hugh Darwen (1998) *Foundation of Object/Relational Databases, The Third Manifesto*. Addison-Wesley, Longman Publishing Co., Inc., Redwood City, CA, USA.

Eilenburg, S. and S. Mac Lane (1945) 'General Theory of Natural Equivalences', *Transactions of the American Mathematical Society*, vol. 58, pp. 231–94.

Murata, Makoto (2000) *Hedge Automata: A Formal Model for XML Schemata*, available at http://www.xml.gr.jp/relax/hedge_nice.html, accessed December 2002.

Rossiter, Nick, David Nelson and Michael Heather (2001) *A Universal Technique for Relating Heterogeneous Data Models*, paper presented at 3rd International Conference on Enterprise Information Systems, Setubal, Portugal, July.

Stonebraker, Michael and Dorothy Moore (1996) *Object-Relational DBMSs: The Next Great Wave*. Morgan Kaufmann Publishers, San Francisco, CA, USA.

University Corporation for Atmospheric Research (2002) *COMET, Multimedia Database Homepage*, available at http://archive.comet.ucar.edu/moria/index.jsp, accessed December 2002.

W3C (2001) *W3C Math Home: What is MathML?*, available at www.w3.org/Math/, accessed December 2002.

Chapter 12
SQL workbook and tutorial

Chapter summary

In Chapter 9 we had a brief introduction to SQL, looked at some of the commands and noted the differences between Oracle SQL and Microsoft Jet SQL used in Access. In this chapter we will take matters considerably further in working through a detailed tutorial on SQL. The first task will be to build the database using only SQL DDL commands. We will then explore many of SQL's DML commands in order to interrogate a database and achieve some useful results.

This tutorial, although completely rewritten and with a different database example, is based on the original work for an Oracle SQL*PLUS tutorial written by Sue Stirk of the University of Sunderland.

Learning outcomes

After studying this chapter, you should check your knowledge against the outcomes below and test your achievement by answering the questions at the end of the chapter. You should be able to:

Outcome 1: Construct a database using SQL DDL commands.
You should be able to create tables and build relationships using SQL data definition commands.

Outcome 2: Interrogate a database using SQL DML commands.
You should be able to use some of the SQL data manipulation commands to add data and construct both simple and complex queries using some SQL functions available within the language.

How will you be assessed on this?

Most SQL exams are machine-based rather than written. Certainly you may well be asked basic syntax queries in a written exam but the construction of complex queries relies on feedback given both in terms of what you can see on the tables generated as well as from the errors generated with no tables.

This chapter has been organised into two sections. The first builds a database using only SQL commands. The remainder of the chapter is an SQL tutorial workbook taking you systematically through many aspects of the SQL language. There are questions included in each of the sections of this tutorial rather than at the end of the chapter as was done in other chapters. (However, we have kept the answers until the end of the chapter, just in case you feel tempted to look.) You are encouraged to experiment with the language to aid your understanding.

Section 1

Building the database

It is advisable during this tutorial to use the services of a simple text editor to copy and paste the commands into the Access SQL query window. Typing directly to this window is possible but not advisable, particularly during the database construction phase. In addition, we have also made available a file called VehicleHireBuild.txt on the book website to help speed up this process. If you have any difficulty downloading this file, then it can be created from the data given in the Appendix.

The data presented represents a Vehicle Rental database system. In terms of entities and relationships, these can be represented as in Figure 12.1.

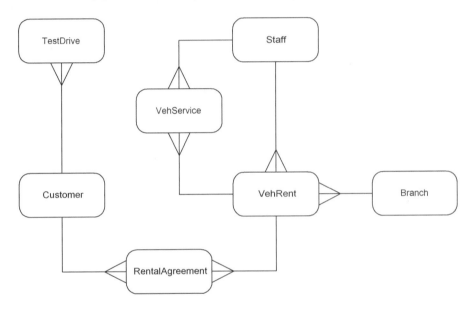

Figure 12.1 Vehicle rental database system

First you should open Microsoft Access and select a Blank Database, naming the project VehicleHire. Select Queries from the list of Objects and double click on 'Create query in Design View'. Close the Show Table dialogue and change the view to SQL View in the View menu.

Separate from the open file, open up a copy of VehicleHireBuild.txt which you will have either downloaded from the book website or typed according to the Appendix. You are now ready to copy and paste over the individual SQL commands.

Before you start entering in the data, you must first create the various tables and relationships. For example, copy the following text from the VehicleHireBuild.txt file over to the SQL View window:

```
create table Customer
(CustomerNo integer not null primary key,
CSurname text(25) Not Null,
CForenames text(25) Not Null,
CStreet text(25) Not Null,
```

CArea text(20),
CTown text(20) not Null,
CPostCode text(8) Not Null,
CTelNo text(12),
CLicenceNo text(16) Not Null,
CMaxRentalPD Currency)

Press the Run command (the exclamation mark on the menu bar).

Access will create the first table called Customer. Leaving the SQL View window still on the screen, confirm that a table called Customer has been created by selecting the Tables object – if necessary selecting 'Refresh' from the View menu as appropriate.

Next copy and paste the next create table instruction to the SQL View window and repeat the process. When all tables have been completed, data can then be added. When you press the Run command after each data entry, a message should appear asking if you wish to append one row of data. Select 'Yes' in all cases.

After all data has been entered it is worth confirming that each table has data associated with it. You are now ready to proceed to the tutorial. The format of the tutorial takes you through various worked examples and constructs. Each section includes sample exercises to carry out on your own.

CRUCIAL TIP

There appears to be a bug within Access with regard to date formats. According to Microsoft documentation, Access should pick up on the regional locale set up in Windows and use this consistently throughout the program. While this is true for the majority of situations, Access does not consistently recognise British dates within an SQL statement. In fact the only time it appears to behave consistently is where the SQL date is meaningless according to the American format. Unfortunately the only workaround that would appear to be consistent is in the mandatory use of American dates in all SQL statements. Output is correct, however, according to the set locale.

Section 2

SQL tutorial workbook

SQL tutorial – Part 1

In this the first of three tutorial blocks, you will learn to construct basic SQL queries.

Learning outcomes

Outcome 1: Retrieve basic data from a table using the SELECT command.

Outcome 2: Retrieve distinct values from a table.

Outcome 3: Carry out basic arithmetic operations using the SELECT command.

Outcome 4: Use of an alias within a query.

Outcome 5: Use of concatenated fields and literals.

Outcome 6: Sort within a query.

Special note

Unless specifically told otherwise you will be using the SQL View window which is part of Access's Query options. You are advised to utilise a text editor such as

NotePad not only to allow for easy editing but also as a means of storing your answers for later recall. To activate a query simply copy the query from the editor and paste into the SQL window.

Selecting all columns

select * from Customer

Activating this query should produce the response shown in Figure 12.2. Note that this is identical to the data currently held in the Customer Table.

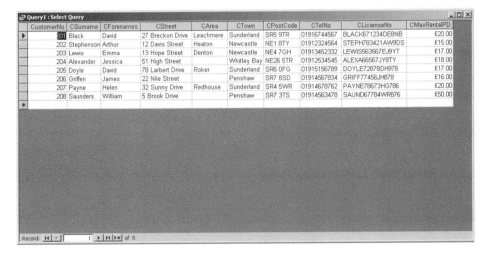

Figure 12.2 Select query response

Access makes no difference between upper and lower case except within a literal string and so the following command would produce the same results:

SELECT * from CUSTOMER

Access also allows you to terminate the command with a semi-colon. This has no effect within Access but is more commonly used to terminate a command in Oracle SQL*Plus.

Selecting columns within a table

There will be many times when selecting all fields from a table will simply swamp us with information rather than highlight only what is necessary. To select one specific column we can use the command:

select CSurname from Customer

If we wanted to display more than one field, then this is achieved by listing the fields out separated by commas, such as:

select CSurname, CForenames from Customer

Selecting unique or distinct values from a table

Sometimes when we make a query we are only interested in unique information. Let us say we wished to know where our customer came from. We could write:

select CTown from Customer

This results in multiple listings of the most popular towns. Although clearly correct it is superfluous in the context of what we were actually looking for. It would be

119

much better to slightly alter the query to give us only the desired information without repetition, particularly if this was a large database with many towns:

select distinct CTown from Customer

Simple arithmetic operations on columns

SQL allows the construction of calculated columns to take place using the basic arithmetic operators. The symbols used are as follows:

Operation	Symbol
Multiply	*
Divide	/
Add	+
Subtract	—

In case of any confusion, the normal 'rules of precedence' applies. This means that in a situation such as:

A+B*C

multiplication and division take precedence over addition and subtraction.

This would be the same as saying A+(B*C).

Use of brackets is permitted to change the order of precedence such as:

(A+B)*C

Let us use the arithmetic operators to create a calculated field. For example, what would the cost of each vehicle be for five days' hire (including the cost of insurance)?

We can get the cost of a daily hire and daily insurance from the VehRent table. To calculate the five-day charge we could use the following:

select VehMake, VehModel, (VehRentPD+VehInsPD)*5
from VehRent

It is also worth noting here that SQL queries ignore white space. As queries gradually expand in terms of size and complexity it is common practice to break the query into lines. We will make use of this feature in our presentation of SQL queries.

Custom table header

In the last query you may have noticed that the returned query simply calls the calculated field an expression in the header row. It would be useful if we could give this column a more helpful name.

This is achieved through the use of an alias or alternative name. To use an alias simply follow the expression with 'AS' followed by the alias name. For example, rewrite the previous query to the following:

select VehMake, VehModel, (VehRentPD+VehInsPD)*5 as [5-Day Charge]
from VehRent

Notice here the mandatory use of square brackets to act as a field delimiter due to the fact that the field name contains a space. If no spaces are used, then there is no need to use the square brackets.

Of course, we can make the whole table more readable by using an alias for every column as in:

```
select VehMake as Make, VehModel as Model,
(VehRentPD + VehInsPD) * 5 as [5-Day Charge]
from VehRent
```

Concatenation

Although we have stored values in separate fields within the database, there are times when it is convenient to concatenate two or more fields together to form a composite output. An example could be a person's name. Take, for example, a situation where we may want to concatenate the Customer's forename followed by a space followed by their Surname. This would be achieved using the '&' concatenation operator as in:

```
select CForenames & ' ' & CSurname as Name
from Customer
```

Use of string literals

In the last example we introduced a space between forename and surname. We needn't stop at just a space, we could introduce a whole sentence if we wished such as:

```
select "The Customer's name is " & CForenames & ' ' & CSurname as Name
from Customer
```

Some things worth noting here relate to the use of single or double inverted commas. Typically these are interchangeable although it is common practice to use the single inverted comma. However, in a situation, as we have here, where we wish to include a single inverted comma (or apostrophe) in the literal text, then use of double inverted commas resolves this problem. If for any reason you wish to include a literal passage in quotations (using double inverted commas, then this is also possible using three sets of double inverted commas, thus:

```
select """"The Customer's name is"""" " & CForenames & ' ' & CSurname as Name
from Customer
```

Sorting of rows in a query

With a limited number of rows, the whole issue of sorting may appear questionable but with large databases and the possibility of many rows being returned by a query, the whole issue of sorting becomes very important.

Consider the following:

```
select VehMake, VehModel, VehCC
from VehRent
order by VehCC desc
```

This will provide a list of all cars available for rental in descending engine size order. SQL provides a means to sort in either ascending or descending order. If nothing is specified, the ascending is taken as the default.

Of course several of the cars have the same engine size and it may be advantageous to sort by more than one criterion. The following query sorts first according to engine descending, then by make in ascending order:

```
select VehMake, VehModel, VehCC
from VehRent
order by VehCC desc, VehMake
```

SQL also allows the use of numbered columns instead of column names when referring to selected fields within an SQL statement. For example, we could have shortened this to:

```
select VehMake, VehModel, VehCC
from VehRent
order by 3 desc, 1
```

It is worth noting at this stage that ordering can also apply to real or calculated columns. It does not apply to aliases (unlike Oracle). Hence if you wish to order on an alias or calculated column, the order statement must refer back to the original columns:

```
Select VehMake, VehModel, (VehRentPD + VehInsPD) * 5 as [5 day Cost]
From VehRent
Order by (VehRentPD + VehInsPD) desc, VehMake
```

Questions on SQL tutorial – Part 1
(Answers are given later in this chapter.)

1. Extract the street names of all customers.

2. Extract the surnames and forenames of all staff.

3. From the list of vehicles for hire, extract a list of their vehicle makes without listing any make twice.

4. List the make, model and total daily hire charge for each vehicle assuming all customers require insurance.

5. List all vehicle registration numbers, the daily cost to hire (without insurance) and the projected cost to rent the same class of vehicle next year assuming inflation costs of 4 per cent

6. Write the SQL query that will yield the table shown in Figure 12.3.

Query1 : Select Query

Hire Information
Vehicle 1002 was hired from 12/03/2002 to 17/03/2002
Vehicle 1007 was hired from 15/03/2002 to 16/03/2002
Vehicle 1001 was hired from 15/03/2002 to 14/04/2002
Vehicle 1006 was hired from 19/03/2002 to 25/03/2002
Vehicle 1008 was hired from 25/03/2002 to 26/03/2002
Vehicle 1002 was hired from 26/03/2002 to 30/04/2002
Vehicle 1010 was hired from 28/03/2002 to 30/03/2002
Vehicle 1005 was hired from 01/04/2002 to 08/04/2002
Vehicle 1015 was hired from 02/04/2002 to 04/04/2002
Vehicle 1002 was hired from 06/04/2002 to 10/04/2002
Vehicle 1002 was hired from 12/04/2002 to 15/04/2002
Vehicle 1003 was hired from 12/04/2002 to 14/04/2002
Vehicle 1005 was hired from 15/04/2002 to 20/04/2002
Vehicle 1007 was hired from 18/04/2002 to 25/04/2002
Vehicle 1002 was hired from 20/04/2002 to 22/04/2002

Figure 12.3 Query results

7. Write the SQL query that will produce a table containing the following data for each Customer:
   – David Black's address is 27 Breckon Drive in Sunderland;
   – Arthur Stephenson's address is 12 Davis Street in Newcastle, etc.

8. Write the SQL query to display the vehicle make, the model, the daily rental and daily insurance costs in order of ascending rental within ascending insurance costs.

SQL tutorial – Part 2

In this the second of three tutorial blocks you will learn to construct more complex SQL queries.

Learning outcomes

Outcome 1: Use the WHERE operator to locate some specific records.

Outcome 2: Use comparison and logical operators in SQL queries.

Outcome 3: Obtain a set of records using the BETWEEN, IN and LIKE operators.

Outcome 4: Use SQL numeric functions.

Outcome 5: Use SQL string functions.

Outcome 6: Use SQL date functions.

Outcome 7: Use SQL group functions.

In the first tutorial we looked primarily at columns or data fields and how these are manipulated. In this tutorial we are going to concentrate more on rows, primarily to see how we can use SQL to limit the number of rows being produced to give a more targeted solution.

The simple WHERE statement

```
select * from VehRent
where VehRentPD = 16
```

The use of the WHERE statement can dramatically reduce the options returned by the query. When used in conjunction with the '=' operator it targets very specific conditions. Other times we may prefer a more pragmatic and less targeted question to find a range of options. SQL has a whole series of comparison operators as follows:

Symbol	Interpretation
=	Is equal to
>	Is greater than
<	Is less than
< >	Is not equal to
> =	Greater than or equal to
< =	Less than or equal to
Between	Between two values

Let us use these to revise the above query as follows:

```
select * from VehRent
```

where VehRentPD < 16

Try out all forms of comparison to ensure you fully understand the output is as expected.

String equality

Of course the equality applies not only to numbers but to strings as well. Hence it is perfectly acceptable to have the following query:

```
select CSurname, CForenames, CTown
from Customer
where CTown = 'Sunderland'
```

Logical operators

SQL also supports combination logic using the Boolean algebra operators AND, OR, XOR and NOT.

Take for example the following query:

```
select VehMake, VehModel, VehColour, VehRentPD
from VehRent
where VehColour = 'Red'
and VehRentPD < 24
```

Compare this to the output from the following query:

```
select VehMake, VehModel, VehColour, VehRentPD
from VehRent
where VehColour = 'Red'
or VehRentPD < 24
```

In the first case both conditions has to be fulfilled whereas in the second, either condition has to be fulfilled returning a much greater selection.

In the next example we see the use of the logical NOT operator:

```
select VehMake, VehModel, VehColour, VehRentPD
from VehRent
where VehColour = 'Red'
and not VehRentPD < 24
```

Here we are still saying the vehicle has to be red but in addition it must not be less than £24 per day to rent.

CRUCIAL TIP

SQL follows the normal rules of precedence with regard to how statements are interpreted and executed. Where you are in any doubt, it is always safer to use parenthesis (brackets) to force precedence.

Thus the last SQL statement could equally have been written as:

```
select VehMake, VehModel, VehColour, VehRentPD
from VehRent
where VehColour = 'Red'
and not (VehRentPD < 24)
```

This arguably makes for easier understanding.

Specifying a range of values

Sometimes it is easier to specify a range of values as in the following:

```
select VehMake, VehModel, VehColour, VehRentPD
from VehRent
where VehRentPD > = 17
and VehRentPD < = 30
```

However, SQL provides an easier option using the BETWEEN operator as in:

```
select VehMake, VehModel, VehColour, VehRentPD
from VehRent
where VehRentPD between (17 and 30)
```

Another approach could be to use specific comparisons as in the following:

```
select VehMake, VehModel, VehColour, VehRentPD
from VehRent
where VehMake = 'Ford'
or VehMake = 'Audi'
or VehMake = 'Lexus'
```

SQL provides a shortcut method also for this type of construct with the IN operator, as in the following:

```
select VehMake, VehModel, VehColour, VehRentPD
from VehRent
where VehMake IN ('Ford', 'Audi', 'Lexus')
```

Wildcard query

SQL provides a way of carrying out a query using a wildcard instead of exact string to effect a comparison:

```
select VehMake, VehModel, VehColour, VehRentPD
from VehRent
where VehMake LIKE 'P*'
```

It should be noted here that Access uses the * for wildcards much the same as it does for Windows. Oracle uses the % symbol for the same purpose.

Built-in functions

As well as the selection functions already discussed, Access contains a whole plethora of useful functions which can be used to build up calculated fields.

For a complete list of functions, check out the Expression Builder in Microsoft Access. This can be accessed from several places: for example, right click a field in Query Design View and select Build.

Access divides functions into many categories such as Arrays, Conversion, Database, Date/Time, DDE/OLE, Domain Aggregate, Error Handling, Financial, General, Input/ Output, Inspection, Math, Messages, Program Flow, SQL Aggregate and Text. There are far too many to go through in detail within the scope of this tutorial but we will highlight a few of the more interesting to discuss.

Round function

There are many times when it is convenient to display a reduced number of decimal places in the output query. For example, consider the following calculation of monthly salary for each member of staff:

```
Select round(SSalary/12, 1)
from Staff
```

This rounds the output to one decimal place.

String handling functions

It is often convenient to display only part of a string rather than the whole string. Access provides three functions to achieve this, namely Left, Mid or Right.

Consider an example where you wish to output only the Customer's Forename initial followed by his surname:

```
Select left(CForenames,1) & '. ' & CSurname as Name
From Customer
```

Note that the number signifies the length of string to be selected. In the case of Access's Mid statement, two numbers are required as in:

```
Select Mid(CForenames, 2, 3)
From Customer
```

Although this statement may not have much meaning in this context, it illustrates the point that it extracts a string starting at position 2, the length of the string being 3 characters.

LCase function

Sometimes we may wish to force a string to be lower case only. This is achieved using the LCase function as in:

```
Select lcase(CSurname)
From Customer
```

UCase function

Similarly, we may wish to force a string to be upper case only. This is achieved using the UCase function as in:

```
Select CSurname, Ctown
From Customer
Where UCase(CTown) = 'NEWCASTLE'
```

Date functions

Access has many date functions useful to SQL queries:

```
Select * from RentalAgreement
Where EndDate = Date()
```

Presently this SQL query will return nothing due to the fact that there is currently nothing out on hire. Simply introduce a further entry in the RentalAgreement table with today's date being the date the agreement is due to expire. Now re-run the SQL query – this should show that a car is due back today.

DateAdd function

Access allows you to add a preset time interval to a date. For example, if we wished to set up a query to give us the dates exactly six months after the start of a hire, we could write:

```
Select AgreeNo, StartDt, DateAdd('m', 6, StartDt) as [6-Month]
From RentalAgreement
```

Notice the interval has been set to months (i.e. 'm'). Equally well this could be set to days, weeks, quarters, years, etc.

DateDiff function

Sometimes it is helpful to be able to calculate the difference between two dates. Let us compute the number of weeks since the end of a rental agreement:

```
Select AgreeNo, DateDiff('w', EndDate, Date()) as Interval
From RentalAgreement
```

Aggregate or group functions

So far we have only considered individual functions. However there are also functions that act on the data as a group.

Avg function

Clearly when we are talking about an average we are talking about something that applies to a group of numbers:

```
Select avg(RentPD) as [Average Rental]
From RentalAgreement
```

Max function

Similar to the Avg function, there can only be one Max result (even although it may apply to more than one row):

```
Select max(RentPD) as [Maximum Rental]
From RentalAgreement
```

Min function

Similar to the Max function:

```
Select min(RentPD) as [Minimum Rental]
From RentalAgreement
```

Count function

Simply counts up the number of applicable rows of data:

```
Select count(CustomerNo) as [No of Customers]
From Customer
```

Sum function

The Sum function is used to give a totalised count of applicable rows of data:

```
Select sum(SSalary) as [Total Staff Salaries]
From Staff
```

GROUP BY clause

While the previous functions carried out calculations on every applicable instance within the group, there are times when it is desirable to produce sub-totals within a query. This is the prime purpose of the GROUP BY clause. There are two important rules to be observed when using the GROUP BY clause:

- Each item in the select statement must be single valued within a group.
- Columns used in the select statement must reappear in the GROUP BY clause (unless these are only used within the group function).

Consider the following:

```
select BranchNo, count(staffno) as [No of Staff], sum(SSalary) as [Branch Salary]
from staff
group by BranchNo
```

Here we are generating both the number of staff as well as the total salary for each branch.

HAVING clause

The HAVING clause is used in conjunction with the GROUP BY clause to limit the number of sub-groups that appear. It is similar to the WHERE clause which applies to individual rows. The HAVING clause, however, applies to groups.

In the case of the last example, let us restrict the branches to those with more than one member of staff at the branch:

```
select BranchNo, count(staffno) as [No of Staff], sum(SSalary) as [Branch Salary]
from staff
group by BranchNo
Having count(StaffNo) > 1
```

Questions on SQL tutorial – Part 2

(Answers are given later in this chapter.)

1. Display a list (make and model) of all non-Ford cars in the hire fleet.

2. Display a list (make and model) of all German cars (BMW, Mercedes-Benz, Audi, and Porsche) in the hire fleet.

3. Display a list (AgreeNo, VehicleNo and CustomerNo) of all vehicle hires where there was a deposit of more than £20 and payment was made by plastic card (i.e. a P on the table)

4. Display a list of customer's surnames and town who do not live in either Penshaw or Whitley Bay.

5. Display the average deposit made on all cars hired.

6. Display the total rent charged to all customers (i.e. RentPD times the number of days hired).

7. Display the total income received from each vehicle in the hire fleet.

8. Display the branch number and number of vehicles dealt with by each branch.

SQL tutorial – Part 3

In this the third of three tutorial blocks, you will learn to construct multi-table SQL queries.

Learning outcomes

Outcome 1: Write an SQL query to join two tables.

Outcome 2: Write an SQL query to join more than two queries.

Outcome 3: Understand the dangers of a Cartesian product.

Outcome 4: Write a single-row multi-query.

Outcome 5: Write a multi-row sub-query.

Joining tables

So far all our queries could be achieved by only one table. However, this is unusual. Most queries will require information to come from different tables.

In Chapter 2 we introduced the concept of a JOIN in order to create a composite set of data with which we could query. We will now see the effect of such a Join.

Consider only some of the fields pertaining to the tables for Branch and Staff (see Tables 12.1 and 12.2):

Table 12.1 Branch	
BranchNo	**BTown**
11	Sunderland
12	Peterlee
13	Newcastle
14	Hexham

Table 12.2 Staff		
BranchNo	**StaffNo**	**SSurname**
11	101	Downey
11	102	Smith
12	103	Harvey
12	104	Marshall
13	105	James
13	106	Tully
14	107	Times

- in the Branch table (Table 12.1), BranchNo is the primary key;
- in the Staff table (Table 12.2), BranchNo is a foreign key.

SQL can perform a join between these two tables, thus:

```
Select branch.BranchNo, BTown, StaffNo, SSurname
From branch, staff
Where branch.BranchNo = staff.BranchNo
```

This creates the output shown in Figure 12.4. This shows clearly that a join has taken place around BranchNo.

	BranchNo	BTown	StaffNo	SSurname
	11	Sunderland	101	Downey
	11	Sunderland	102	Smith
	12	Peterlee	103	Harvey
	12	Peterlee	104	Marshall
	13	Newcastle	105	James
	13	Newcastle	106	Tully
▶	14	Hexham	107	Times

Figure 12.4 Join results

Notice that we had to introduce both table names when referring to BranchNo as this would otherwise have been ambiguous.

An alternative approach is to use aliases where we shorten the table name perhaps even to a single letter just for the duration of the query, such as:

```
Select b.BranchNo, b.BTown, s.StaffNo, s.SSurname
From branch b, staff s
Where b.BranchNo = s.BranchNo
```

This produces an identical result but may be easier to write.

CRUCIAL TIP

Do not forget to define the aliases in the FROM clause before you use it in the WHERE clause. Use of the alias in the SELECT clause only happens if you require that column to be part of the query. It is a common error to forget to define the aliases.

Joining more than two tables

Of course you will often be faced with the situation where you will be required to join more than two tables. Invariably this will involve a more complex query requiring use of the logical operators AND and OR.

Consider the situation where we need to combine elements of Branch, Staff as well as the VehRent tables:

    Select b.BranchNo, b.BTown, s.StaffNo, v.VehReg
    From branch b, staff s, VehRent v
    Where b.BranchNo=s.BranchNo AND s.StaffNo=v.StaffNo

In this case two joins were necessary, one to join Staff and Branch, the other to join Staff and VehReg.

Cartesian product

This was originally mentioned in Chapter 2 but has great significance when carrying out joins. If you join incorrectly and do not specify the basis of the join, this will produce the famous Cartesian product, i.e. A table with 4 rows (Branch), joined to a table with 7 rows (Staff) joined to a table of 15 rows (VehRent) can potentially produce a joined table of $4 \times 7 \times 15 = 420$ entries.

Try this for proof:

    Select b.BranchNo, b.BTown, s.StaffNo, v.VehReg
    From branch b, staff s, VehRent v

All we have done here is to forget to specify the terms of the join.

While this may seem like a game, remember we are dealing with very small databases here. Even so, we have the potential of producing a Cartesian product of $4 \times 7 \times 15 \times 8 \times 15 \times 6 \times 5 = 1,512,000$ records if we linked all tables.

On a production database with considerably more records and tables, producing a Cartesian product could easily tie up computers for hours senselessly churning out something that is essentially useless. Beware!

Sub-queries

There are many instances where data cannot be directly obtained from a query but requires at least one further query to be resolved before the main query can be addressed. Take, for example, the apparently simple query, name all cars more expensive to hire than a Mercedes-Benz. Before we can answer that question, we would need to know the cost of hiring a Mercedes-Benz. Once we have this information, the main query can be easily resolved. This type of problem can be resolved though the use of a nested structure or sub-query.

The basic format of the sub-query is:

    Select column 1, column 2, etc
    From table
    Where column =
      (select column
      from table
      where condition);

Let us go back to our original query, namely that we want a list of all cars more expensive to hire than a Mercedes-Benz:

    Select VehMake, VehModel, VehRentPD
    From VehRent

```
Where VehRentPD >
   (select VehRentPD
   from VehRent
   where VehMake='MercedesBenz')
```

Here the inner nested structure is evaluated first to get the cost of hire for the Mercedes-Benz. This is then used in the outer structure query to obtain a list of all cars whose cost to rent is greater.

Let us look at another example here involving more than one table. Assume we wish a list of all staff who work in Sunderland. As we cannot guarantee that staff working in Sunderland actually live in Sunderland, we first have to get the branch number for Sunderland from the Branch table before we look to see which staff work at that Branch number:

```
Select StaffNo, SForenames, SSurname
From Staff
Where BranchNo =
   (select BranchNo
   from Branch
   where BTown='Sunderland')
```

In this case the sub-query returns one row of one field.

Technically, we do not need to write this as a sub-query. We could take the decision to join the branch and staff table before looking for employees who work in Sunderland. This could be achieved using the following:

```
Select StaffNo, SForenames, SSurname
From staff s, branch b
where s.BranchNo=b.BranchNo AND BTown='Sunderland'
```

Sub-queries that return more than one row
So far we have only considered simple sub-queries but these can also return multiple rows if required. Consider the situation where we wish to determine the highest salary paid at each branch.

```
Select SForenames, SSurname, SSalary, BranchNo
From staff
Where SSalary in
   (select max(SSalary)
   from staff
   group by BranchNo)
```

Ordering data in sub-queries
One of the problems with sub-queries is that the ORDER BY clause is not allowed to appear as part of the sub-query. Instead it should appear as the last statement of the outer query.

```
Select VehMake, VehModel, VehReg
From VehRent
Where BranchNo=
   (select BranchNo
   from Branch
   where BTown='Peterlee')
order by VehMake desc
```

Exists or not exists

The clauses EXISTS or NOT EXISTS can be used for sub-queries to produce a Boolean result (True or False).

For example, to find all vehicles based at Sunderland, we could use:

```
Select VehMake, Vehmodel, VehReg
From VehRent v
Where exists
  (select *
  from branch b
  where v.BranchNo = b.BranchNo and BTown = 'Sunderland')
```

Again for this example we could have used a JOIN as in:

```
Select VehMake, VehModel, VehReg
From VehRent v, Branch b
Where v.BranchNo = b.BranchNo and BTown = 'Sunderland'
```

Questions on SQL tutorial – Part 3

(Answers are given later in this chapter.)

1. Find the vehicle registration, make and model of the most expensive car to hire in the fleet.

2. Find the car registration, make and model of the most expensive car to rent at each branch. Display the result in descending order of cost.

3. Find the other numbers of all cars held at the same branch as vehicle registration no. T23 TRD

4. Show the following detail of all cars which cost less to rent than the average rental cost for that branch:

   – Car Registration No, Branch Name, Cost to Rent, Avg Branch Rental costs

5. Display the following information for the Branch with the highest car rental cost

   – BranchNo, Sum(Staff Salary at that Branch)

Answers to SQL tutorial – Part 1

1. Select CStreet
   from Customer

2. Select SSurname, SForenames
   from Staff

3. Select distinct VehMake
   from VehRent

4. Select VehMake, VehModel, VehRentPD + VehInsPD
   as [Total Daily Hire Charge]
   from VehRent

5. Select VehReg, VehRentPD, VehRentPD * 1.04 as [Projected Cost]
   from VehRent

   Note that this projected cost calculation does not default to a currency. You may therefore wish to force the solution to a currency using the built-in conversion function CCur. This would change the solution to:
   Select VehReg, VehRentPD, CCur(VehRentPD * 1.04) as [Projected Cost]
   from VehRent

6. Select 'Vehicle ' & VehicleNo & ' was hired from ' & StartDt & ' to ' &
   EndDate as [Hire Information]
   From RentalAgreement

7. Select CForenames & ' ' & CSurname & '''s address is ' & CStreet & ' in ' &
   CTown
   From Customer

8. Select VehMake, VehModel, VehRentPD, VehInsPD
   from VehRent
   order by VehRentPD, VehInsPD desc

Answers to SQL tutorial – Part 2

1. Select VehMake, VehModel
   from VehRent
   where VehMake <> 'Ford'

2. Select VehMake, VehModel
   from VehRent
   where VehMake in ('BMW', 'MercedesBenz', 'Audi', 'Porsche')

3. Select AgreeNo, VehicleNo, CustomerNo
   from RentalAgreement
   where DepAmount > 20 and PayMethod = 'P'

4. Select CSurname, CTown
   from Customer
   where CTown not in ('Penshaw', 'Whitley Bay')

5. Select Avg(DepAmount) as [Average Deposit]
   from RentalAgreement

6. Select RentPD * (DateDiff('d', StartDt, EndDate)) as [Total Rent Charged]
   from RentalAgreement

   We assume here that customers obey the usual rules of hire where a car can be
   picked up in the afternoon of the first day of hire and dropped off early morning
   of the last day of hire. If not then we would need to add one to the difference
   date calculation.

7. Select VehicleNo, Sum(RentPD * (DateDiff('d', StartDt, EndDate)))
        as [Total Income Received]
   from RentalAgreement
   Group by VehicleNo

8. Select BranchNo, Count(VehicleNo) as [Number of Vehicles]
   from VehRent
   Group by BranchNo

Answers to SQL tutorial – Part 3

1. Select VehReg, VehMake, VehModel
   from VehRent
   where VehRentPD =
      (select max(VehRentPD)
      from VehRent)

2. Select VehReg, VehMake, VehModel, BranchNo, VehRentPD
   from VehRent
   where VehRentPD in
      (select max(VehRentPD)
      from VehRent
      Group by BranchNo)
   order by VehRentPD desc

3. Select VehReg
   From VehRent
   Where BranchNo =
      (Select BranchNo
      from VehRent
      where VehReg = 'T23 TRD')
   and VehReg <> 'T23 TRD'

Note the last line has been introduced to exclude Registration No. T23 TRD. The question asks only for the other numbers.

4. Select VehReg, BTown, VehRentPD
   from VehRent v, Branch b
   where V.BranchNo = b.BranchNo AND VehRentPD <
      (select avg(VehRentPD)
      from VehRent
      where BranchNo = v.BranchNo)

Note here the need to join the BranchNo of the inner select to the BranchNo of the outer select. This is called a correlated sub-query where the sub-query is dependent on the current row of the main query.

5. Select branchNo, sum(SSalary) as [Staff Salary at Branch]
   from staff
   group by BranchNo
   having BranchNo =
      (Select BranchNo
      from VehRent
      where VehRentPD =
         (select max(VehRentPD)
         from VehRent))

Note here the use of three select statements. The inner loop finds the most expensive vehicle to hire. The middle loop finds the BranchNo for that vehicle. The outer loop finds the total of staff salaries at that Branch.

Appendix
Data for SQL tutorial

The following file *VehicleHireBuild.txt* is available for download from the book website.

Tables (with relationships)

Create Table Customer
(CustomerNo integer not null primary key,
CSurname text(25) Not Null,
CForenames text(25) Not Null,
CStreet text(25) Not Null,
CArea text(20),
CTown text(20) not Null,
CPostCode text(8) Not Null,
CTelNo text(12),
CLicenceNo text(16) Not Null,
CMaxRentalPD Currency)

Create Table Staff
(StaffNo integer Not Null primary key,
BranchNo integer Not Null,
SSurname text(25) Not Null,
SForenames text(25) Not Null,
SStreet text(25) Not Null,
SArea text(20),
STown text(20) not Null,
SPostCode text(8) Not Null,
STelNo text(12),
SGender text(1),
SSalary currency)

Create Table Branch
(BranchNo integer Not Null primary Key,
BStreet text(25) Not Null,
BArea text(20),
BTown text(20) not Null,
BPostCode text(8) Not Null,
BTelNo text(12))

Create Table VehRent
(VehicleNo integer Not Null primary key,
VehReg text (8) Not Null,
VehMake text(12) Not Null,
VehModel text(12) Not Null,
VehCC text(8) Not Null,
VehGearType text(1) Not Null,
VehColour text(12) Not Null,

VehSeats integer Not Null,
VehRentPD currency Not Null,
VehInsPD currency,
StaffNo integer Not Null references Staff(StaffNo),
BranchNo integer Not Null references Branch(BranchNo),
Available text(1),
RComments text(150))

Create Table RentalAgreement
(AgreeNo integer Not Null primary key,
VehicleNo integer Not Null references VehRent(VehicleNo),
CustomerNo integer Not Null references Customer(CustomerNo),
RentPD currency,
PayMethod text(1) Not Null,
DepAmount currency,
DepPaid text(1),
StartDt Datetime Not Null,
EndDate DateTime)

Create Table TestDrive
(VehicleNo integer Not Null,
CustomerNo integer Not Null references Customer(CustomerNo),
TestDate datetime,
DComments text(50),
primary key (VehicleNo, CustomerNo))

Create Table VehService
(VehicleNo integer Not Null references VehRent(VehicleNo),
StaffNo integer Not Null references Staff(StaffNo),
ServiceDate datetime Not Null,
SComments text(150),
primary key(VehicleNo, StaffNo, ServiceDate))

Table data

insert into Customer
values (201, 'Black', 'David', '27 Breckon Drive', 'Leachmere', 'Sunderland', 'SR5 9TR', '01916744567', 'BLACK671234DE8NB', 20)

insert into Customer
values (202, 'Stephenson', 'Arthur', '12 Davis Street', 'Heaton', 'Newcastle', 'NE1 8TY', '01912324564', 'STEPH783421AW9DS', 15)

insert into Customer
values (203, 'Lewis', 'Emma', '13 Hope Street', 'Denton', 'Newcastle', 'NE4 7GH', '01913452332', 'LEWIS563567EJ9YT', 17)

insert into Customer
values (204, 'Alexander', 'Jessica', '51 High Street', NULL, 'Whitley Bay', 'NE26 5TR', '01912534545', 'ALEXA66567JY8TY', 18)

insert into Customer
values (205, 'Doyle', 'David', '78 Larbert Drive', 'Roker', 'Sunderland', 'SR6 0FG', '01915156789', 'DOYLE72878DH978', 17)

insert into customer
values (206, 'Griffen', 'James', '22 Nile Street', NULL, 'Penshaw', 'SR7 8SD', '01914567834', 'GRIFF77456JH878', 16)

insert into customer
values (207, 'Payne', 'Helen', '32 Sunny Drive', 'Redhouse', 'Sunderland', 'SR4 5WR', '01914678762', 'PAYNE78673HG786', 20)

insert into customer
values (208, 'Saunders', 'William', '5 Brook Drive', NULL, 'Penshaw', 'SR7 3TS', '01914563478', 'SAUND67784WR876', 50)

insert into staff
values (101, 11, 'Downey', 'Carol', '21 Regent Terrace', 'Grangetown', 'Sunderland', 'SR2 9YR', '01915670976', 'F', 23000)

insert into staff
values (102, 11, 'Smith', 'James', '11 Mill Lane', 'Fulwell', 'Sunderland', 'SR6 8EW', '01915489867', 'M', 19000)

insert into staff
values (103, 12, 'Harvey', 'David', '19 Burnhope Way', NULL, 'Peterlee', 'SR8 2GH', '01915865543', 'M', 28000)

insert into staff
values (104, 12, 'Marshall', 'June', '35 York Road', NULL, 'Hartlepool', 'TS26 9SD', '01429274245', 'F', 18000)

insert into staff
values (105, 13, 'James', 'Veronica', '23 Victoria Square', 'Jesmond', 'Newcastle', 'NE2 3RE', '01912816856', 'F', 29000)

insert into staff
values (106, 13, 'Tully', 'Peter', '12 Osborne Road', NULL, 'Newcastle', 'NE2 2CB', '01912122300', 'M', 24000)

insert into staff
values (107, 14, 'Times', 'Ian', '32 Leazes Crescent', NULL, 'Hexham', 'NE46 7YT', '01434601976', 'M', 32000)

insert into branch
values (11, '56 High Street', 'Fulwell', 'Sunderland', 'SR4 8UT', '01915143432')

insert into branch
values (12, '32 Wessington Lane', NULL, 'Peterlee', 'SR8 2NY', '01915180292')

insert into branch
values (13, '23 Peters Street', 'Heaton', 'Newcastle', 'NE1 9TR', '01912328345')

insert into branch
values (14, '11 Wright Way', NULL, 'Hexham', 'NE47 5RT', '01434684325')

insert into vehrent
values (1001, 'S51 NGH', 'Ford', 'Mondeo', '2000', 'M', 'Red', 4, 23, 9, 101, 11, 'Y', NULL)

insert into vehrent
values (1002, 'T76 HGH', 'Ford', 'Fiesta', '1600', 'M', 'Blue', 4, 16, 7, 102, 11, NULL, NULL)

insert into vehrent
values (1003, 'R78 RTD', 'BMW', '5-Series', '2500', 'A', 'Silver', 5, 37, 17, 101, 11, 'Y', NULL)

insert into vehrent
values (1004, 'S56 TSG', 'Fiat', 'Brava', '1600', 'M', 'Brown', 4, 19, 9, 102, 11, NULL, NULL)

insert into vehrent
values (1005, 'W67 YTD', 'Nissan', 'Primera', '2000', 'A', 'Silver', 4, 22, 12, 103, 12, 'Y', NULL)

insert into vehrent
values (1006, 'W72 YTD', 'Nissan', 'Almera', '1400', 'M', 'Blue', 4, 16, 6, 103, 12, NULL, NULL)

insert into vehrent
values (1007, 'S67 YFG', 'Peugeot', '406', '1800', 'M', 'Yellow', 4, 21, 12, 104, 12, NULL, NULL)

insert into vehrent
values (1008, 'T89 HJK', 'Proton', 'Persona', '1500', 'M', 'Black', 4, 16, 6, 104, 12, 'Y', NULL)

insert into vehrent
values (1009, 'S45 KLR', 'Mazda', 'Xedos 9', 2300, 'A', 'Grey', 4, 34, 15, 105, 13, 'Y', NULL)

insert into vehrent
values (1010, 'T23 TRD', 'MercedesBenz', 'SLK', '2300', 'A', 'Silver', 2, 30, 14, 105, 13, NULL, NULL)

insert into vehrent
values (1011, 'W56 YFG', 'Audi', 'RS4', '2550', 'M', 'Red', 4, 25, 12, 106, 13, NULL, NULL)

insert into vehrent
values (1012, 'S45 HTR', 'Seat', 'Leon', '1600', 'M', 'Yellow', 4, 16, 8, 106, 13, 'Y', NULL)

insert into vehrent
values (1013, 'T34 URT', 'Skoda', 'Felicia', '1900', 'M', 'Red', 4, 15, 9, 106, 13, NULL, NULL)

insert into vehrent
Values (1014, 'W45 WDF', 'Lexus', 'IS200', '2000', 'A', 'Silver', 4, 25, 11, 107, 14, NULL, NULL)

insert into vehrent
values (1015, 'S42 TJP', 'Porsche', 'Boxster', '2700', 'M', 'White', 2, 38, 19, 107, 14, 'Y', NULL)

insert into rentalagreement
values (2001, 1002, 203, 16, 'P', 50, 'Y', #03/12/2002#, #03/17/2002#)

insert into rentalagreement
values (2002, 1007, 208, 21, 'C', 20, 'Y', #03/15/2002#, #03/16/2002#)

insert into rentalagreement
values (2003, 1001, 205, 19, 'A', 0, 'N', #03/15/2002#, #04/14/2002#)

insert into rentalagreement
values (2004, 1006, 202, 16, 'P', 20, 'Y', #03/19/2002#, #03/25/2002#)

insert into rentalagreement
values (2005, 1008, 203, 16, 'C', 25, 'Y', #03/25/2002#, #03/26/2002#)

insert into rentalagreement
values (2006, 1002, 207, 15, 'A', 0, 'N', #03/26/2002#, #04/30/2002#)

insert into rentalagreement
values (2007, 1010, 206, 25, 'P', 50, 'Y', #03/28/2002#, #03/30/2002#)

insert into rentalagreement
values (2008, 1005, 203, 22, 'P', 20, 'Y', #04/01/2002#, #04/08/2002#)

insert into rentalagreement
values (2009, 1015, 204, 38, 'C', 20, 'Y', #04/02/2002#, #04/04/2002#)

insert into rentalagreement
values (2010, 1002, 201, 16, 'P', 0, 'N', #04/06/2002#, #04/10/2002#)

insert into rentalagreement
values (2011, 1002, 201, 16, 'P', 0, 'N', #04/12/2002#, #04/15/2002#)

insert into rentalagreement
values (2012, 1003, 204, 37, 'P', 50, 'Y', #04/12/2002#, #04/14/2002#)

insert into rentalagreement
values (2013, 1005, 203, 22, 'P', 20, 'Y', #04/15/2002#, #04/20/2002#)

insert into rentalagreement
values (2014, 1007, 202, 21, 'C', 20, 'Y', #04/18/2002#, #04/25/2002#)

insert into rentalagreement
values (2015, 1002, 205, 16, 'P', 20, 'Y', #04/20/2002#, #04/22/2002#)

insert into testdrive
values (1003, 205, #03/14/2002#, 'Nice car but far too expensive')

insert into testdrive
values (1001, 205, #03/15/2002#, 'Good performance')

insert into testdrive
values (1004, 201, #03/17/2002#, 'Not enough leg room in the back')

insert into testdrive
values (1014, 203, #03/21/2002#, 'Nice car, shame about the price')

insert into testdrive
values (1011, 204, #04/01/2002#, 'Do not like the colour')

insert into testdrive
values (1002, 206, #04/02/2002#, 'Car too small')

insert into vehservice
values (1007, 104, #03/17/2002#, 'Routine service')

insert into vehservice
values (1002, 102, #03/18/2002#, 'Check clutch and brake fluid')

insert into vehservice
values (1010, 105, #03/22/2002#, 'Some paintwork scratches to be removed from previous hire')

insert into vehservice
values (1006, 103, #03/27/2002#, 'Major service – check washers')

insert into vehservice
values (1012, 106, #04/01/2002#, 'Routine maintenance')

Glossary

ACID
An acronym used to describe the four key properties of a transaction-based system, namely Atomicity, Consistency, Isolation and Durability.

Ad-hoc query
A query made to the database for information 'on the fly'. This would not have been anticipated explicitly during the design of the database and hence no pre-programmed version of the query would exist.

Aggregate functions
This is the name given to a set of SQL functions that can operate over a range of data. Examples would be Count, Min, Max, Sum, Avg, etc.

Application programming interface (API)
These are defined entry or interface points for connecting application programs to higher order programs such as DBMS, operating systems, etc.

Application software
These are generally complete computer programs written to perform a specific task for an end user. Examples would be accounting programs, sales and order processing programs, etc. Generally these types of programs utilise the services of a DBMS to fulfil their requirements.

ASCII
This is an acronym for the American Standard Code for Information Interchange. This represents an attempt by the ISO to provide a standard coding structure for character interchange. Although largely accepted within PC and minicomputer circles, it is less of a standard with many mainframe companies who created their own standards, such as IBM's EBCDIC (Extended Binary Coded Decimal Interchange Code).

Atomicity
The smallest 'unit' of a transaction as applied to a database. Part of the role of the DBMS is to ensure that such a unit of transaction is either completed in its entirety or aborted leaving the data in its original state.

Attribute
This is normally synonymous with a column in a relational database. It represents a property of an object or entity.

Authentication
Often referred to as 'logging on', this is a security process where the user would be asked to provide, typically, a username and password for identification purposes. This information would be compared to data stored within the system and either allowed to proceed or blocked accordingly.

Backup
In the context of databases, this is the process of taking a copy of the database and storing it in a safe place to enable full restoration should any problem occur. Generally such a backup would be to some form of removable media which could be stored 'off-site'. In the event of a 'disaster' such as a fire or simply data loss

through corruption, the database could be restored to the state it was at time of the backup.

Batch processing
Batch processing consists of entering all data pertaining to a group of transactions to some intermediate form in preparation for entering the whole batch of data into a database. In large systems such as mainframe computers, this technique decreases the 'on-line' time taken to enter the data and was very common in older systems. Nowadays, with increased networking computing, 'on-line' processing is much more common.

Bit
This is a shortened name for 'binary digit' and is the smallest unit of digital information consisting of either '1' or '0'.

B-tree
This is a form of index structure based on a treelike formation. It provides a very efficient algorithm for accessing data records.

Byte
The amount of memory required to store one character of data. Generally accepted as eight bits, the term 'byte' is often referred to as a shortened form of 'by eight'

Candidate key
Where more than one column could be used to uniquely identify the rows in a relational table, these would be termed 'candidate keys'. After selecting which column to use as the primary key, the remaining candidate keys would then be called the alternate keys.

Cardinality
This defines both the maximum and minimum number of occurrences of entities that can take part in a specific relationship. Examples are one-to-one, one-to-many, many-to-many, etc.

Cartesian product
This is normally the undesirable result of joining two or more tables in a query without specifying the join between each pair of tables. Such an action usually results in the return of huge numbers of rows.

Cascading delete
This is a process managed by the DBMS that ensures that, when a row is deleted from a table, all related rows in other tables will also be deleted.

Cascading update
This is a process managed by the DBMS that ensures that, when a row in a table containing the primary key is updated, there will be an equivalent update to all foreign key values in related rows in other tables.

Catalogue
This is a description of the tables used by the DBMS to store information about the various objects within a database. This is often termed metadata.

Client/server
This is a form of distributed computing where two or more computers act cooperatively to carry out a combined process. Typically the client computer will provide a graphical user interface for entering and querying information. The client computer would call on the services of a server computer to carry out much of the information retrieval from data stored centrally on the server computer. Using this approach many clients can share a common database, effectively behaving like a very large centralised computing system but at a fraction of the cost.

Clustering

This is the process of storing related records together on some physical storage device. Essentially the physical storage is made to reflect a particular logical association of data.

Collating sequence

This refers to the way the computer will order a set of records. This is generally a feature of the way the computer will order its own set of printable characters.

Column

In a relational database system, a column is synonymous with an attribute or property of an entity or object.

Command-line interface

This is a user interface that requires entry be made by typed commands. Often termed a 'DOS-style' interface it differs from that of a graphical interface where commands are generally entered though graphical selection, icons, etc.

Commit

This is a keyword in many versions of SQL which is used to make permanent the results of a particular transaction.

Composite key

Sometimes termed a 'concatenated key', this is a key that consists of two or more columns within a table. It is generally used in situations where one column may not be enough to guarantee the uniqueness of a row within a table.

Conceptual data model

A model of the data storage requirements for a given system produced to be independent of the way the data will be physically stored. An entity-relationship diagram would be a typical example of a conceptual model.

Concurrency

This is allowing multiple users to simultaneously access a database. Generally this requires different forms of concurrency control such as record locking to prevent database inconsistency.

Consistency

Changes made to a database as a result of a transaction must be fully reflected throughout the database ensuring that there is no time data can ever be used when it is in an inconsistent or incomplete state.

Constraint

A rule enforced by the DBMS to ensure integrity or consistency of data. For example, if the rule for a column is that it must be 'not null', then the DBMS will ensure that data for a record will not be accepted unless a value for that column has been given.

Correlated sub-query

This is basically a query within a query. By referencing values returned by the outer query, a sub-query will evaluate once for every row returned by the outer query.

CRUD functions

This is an acronym referring to the Create, Read, Update and Delete functions.

Data

This is any form of information or facts regarding items of significance.

Data administrator

This is the person whose job is concerned with the management, planning and documentation of the various information resources within an organisation. It often entails both the creation and enforcing of standards relating to naming and storage of data to ensure the availability, consistency and integrity of the data being held.

Data analysis
This relates to the ability to produce logical models of data from real-world events or scenarios.

Data analyst
This describes a person whose job entails carrying out the various analysis activities associated with database design. This would include requirements analysis and conceptual modelling through to logical database design.

Data conversion
This describes the process of converting data using one method of storage into another. An example would include converting string data to numerical data. Where data is well defined, this process can be very simple but often requires that the resulting converted data has to be 'cleaned up' before it can reliably be used as input data to another system.

Data definition language (DDL)
This describes a language that can be used to define the various parts that constitute a database. An example of this includes SQL which has data definition statements within its syntax (e.g. CREATE TABLE).

Data dictionary
A term used to describe a central repository of information concerning a database. This would include details of all tables, attributes, access rights, etc. It is often referred to as the system catalogue or metadata.

Data integrity
This is the process of ensuring that data is both accurate and relates properly with associated data held elsewhere within the database. It uses all the business rules and constraints to ensure that invalid data cannot be accepted into a database.

Data item
This describes a single piece of information held within a database. It is the smallest unit of storage within a DBMS.

Data manipulation language (DML)
This describes a language that can be used to manipulate the various parts that constitute a database. An example of this includes SQL which has data manipulation statements within its syntax (e.g. SELECT and UPDATE).

Data mining
This describes the process of relating and extracting generally unknown data from often very large databases and using this to make informed management or business decisions.

Data security
This describes the process of securing or protecting data held in computers by different means. This could include physical access, password access or even data encryption.

Data sharing
This describes the process of making data available to more than one user or system.

Data type
This describes the specific type of data acceptable within a field or table column such as date, number or even text. All entries will be checked within the context of their own data type and rejected if incompatible. For example, the system will reject characters in a numeric field or inappropriate dates in a date field.

Data warehouse

This describes a large database system or repository for collection of data in either complete or summary form from many other corporate databases. Using data mining techniques, new relationships, trends and other analysis can take place separate from the feeding databases which are usually optimised for efficient data entry and are less efficient for analysis purposes.

Database

This describes a logical collection of related data stored and maintained for the purposes intended by its creator.

Database administrator

This is the person whose job is concerned with both the implementation and maintenance of databases. This generally involves ensuring that databases are implemented correctly and usefully as well as making sure that these are available as required.

Database management system (DBMS)

This is generally a system used to both create and manage data within databases. It provides the user interface between the user and the data as well as providing tools related to security and integrity of data.

Database server

This provides a means of running a client/server arrangement on a networked arrangement. The database server will provide central data access facilities to allow the various client computers to treat the database as though it is an integral part of their own systems.

Deadlock

Often called 'deadly embrace', this describes the unacceptable situation where one process cannot complete without access to resources currently in use by another process. Similarly the other process cannot also complete until it can access resources in use by the first process. The DBMS has to be aware of such possibilities and either ideally prevent their occurrence or successfully negotiate a conclusion by 'rolling back' transactions as required.

Default value

A valid value entered automatically for a particular field where data is found to be missing. Note that this would have to be specifically declared and could not apply to primary key fields.

Degree

This is used to denote the number of attributes within a relationship. It equates to the number of columns in a relational table.

Denormalisation

This is the deliberate action of introducing some level of redundancy into a database table to enhance the overall performance of the database. Strict adherence to rules of normalisation can often end up requiring a number of joins to achieve a particular view. Denormalisation includes the merging of, say, two tables to save the process necessitating an additional join.

Difference

A relational operator which, when applied to two tables of similar structure, subtracts any common rows leaving the difference between the two tables.

Distributed database

This is a database system whose parts are located on more than one computer connected together by a communications network. This could mean a client/server computer arrangement or indeed the integration of several databases at different sites. The combined effect is for the system to act and behave as one logical unit.

Domain
This represents the range of values within which real attribute values can be stored. This could represent a list of values or details of its upper and lower constraining values.

Encryption
This describes the encoding of data into a form that cannot be understood without the ability to first decrypt the data.

Entity
This is a separately identifiable 'thing of significance' about which we want to keep data and has a relationship with some other entity.

Entity integrity
This describes the requirements for each column in a relation to be separately identifiable and each row to be identifiable by means of a 'non-null' primary key.

Entity-relationship (ER) model
This is a diagrammatical approach to representing both entities as well as the relationships between them. It was proposed originally by Peter Chen in a paper in 1976. ER diagrams may also be used to show the various attributes for each entity.

Entity type
This is the collective name for different instances of an entity. This would normally be expressed in the singular. For example, for an entity called Building we could list many buildings as different instances of the entity.

Equi-join
A relational join between two tables which will leave only the rows where the values match in the join columns of the two tables and are not null.

Expression
A set of mathematical operations which when calculated will produce a result. For example $x^3 = 20 + 7$ is an expression which when calculated would give x the value of 3.

Field
This is a single unit of data within a file, often used to refer to a column within a relational database. A field as such has no value but represents the place or container where the actual data is stored. Thus a field can contain different values at different times.

File
This is a physical area for storing a single organisational unit of data. In terms of a database it is likely to be the physical disk space for the storage of all operational components such as tables, relationships, properties, data, etc.

Foreign key
This is an attribute or field of one table that references the primary key of another table.

Functional dependence
This refers to the implicit bonding that exists between differing attributes within the same entity. For example, in the case of a person, two attributes may be street name and district. Knowing the street name would allow us to deduce the district making the district functionally dependent on the street name.

Graphical user interface (GUI)
This is an interface where graphical objects such as icons, buttons, menus, etc. can give command instruction to an application. An example of this would be Windows.

Homonym
A word used which has different meanings in different places or when used within a different context.

HTML
This is an abbreviation for Hypertext Markup Language adopted by the Worldwide Web Consortium (W3C) as a standard for marking up documents to be published on the Web.

HTTP
This is an abbreviation for Hypertext Transfer protocol, the most common protocol adopted by the Worldwide Web Consortium (W3C) for the transfer of HTML documents over the Internet.

Index
This is a method of mapping logical quantities to physical addresses. This is similar in concept to that of a book index which publishes an organised list from which the reader is pointed to a physical page. Database indexes are used to find the location of specific rows rather than searching through entire tables. They are generally used to speed up both searching and sorting operations

Information
This is essentially data that has been organised in such a way as to be useful or meaningful to the user. It has the basic implication of being useful.

Instance
This is a single occurrence of an entity usually denoted by a single row within a table – see *entity type*.

Integrity constraint
This is a rule used by the DBMS to ensure that data entered is both accurate and applicable – see *data integrity*.

Intersection
A relational operator which when applied to two tables of similar structure leaves the rows that are in both tables.

Join
A relational operator which when applied to two tables produces a combination of the two tables (all rows of one table with all rows in the other) excluding rows with equal values in the join columns.

Kernel
As applied to a DBMS, this concerns the central engine which in turn takes care of all central management functions within the system. This includes functions such as CRUD, data integrity, etc.

Key
A specific column or columns within a database table used to locate records within the database.

Legacy database system
This is generally the name given to an older database application still considered important to the success of a company.

Link entity
This is an artificial entity introduced into an ER diagram to resolve a 'many-to-many' relationship between two existing entities.

Lock
This is a term given to the technique of making certain database records either 'read-only' or inaccessible during the time one user is using the information and which may be subject to subsequent update. This is to prevent a record from being changed by one user while in use by another thus resulting in data inconsistencies.

Logical data independence
This is a feature of a DBMS that allows the physical reorganisation of files making up the database without have to make any changes to application programs using the database. Traditionally such a change would require application programs to be modified and recompiled.

Many-to-many relationship
This is a relationship between two entities that causes difficulty in implementation within a relational database. It implies that many instances of one entity can be related to many instances of another enity.

Metadata
Essentially meaning 'data about data', metadata is sometimes referred to as the data dictionary or system catalogue. It holds data such as relationships, constraints, structure, etc.

Multi-user access
This relates to the simultaneous use of both DBMS and data by more than one user.

Non-procedural query language
A programming language based on what must be done rather than the procedural steps required to execute such an instruction. Structured Query Language (SQL) is a non-procedural query language.

Normalisation
This is a process of making logical associations between the various items of data to ensure that the resulting database design will be free from duplication of data and file maintenance abnormalities.

Null
This is a special representation within a database to represent missing or incomplete data. For example, if an attribute was Cost, then 0 would represent an item with no value. This is different from 'null' which still implies a value albeit one which has yet to be supplied.

Object Query Language (OQL)
A non-procedural programming language used to define, manipulate and query data within an object-oriented database. OQL is modelled on SQL and indeed retains much of the SQL syntax.

Operator
This is a mathematical operation performed on, typically, a numeric, text or logical value. For example, the operator + is used to add two values together to achieve a single solution.

Outer join
A relational operator which when applied to two tables produces a combination in which we keep all the rows from one of the tables irrespective of whether they match or not.

Persistence
This is a characteristic applied to data describing its ability to be held safe for a period of time. Examples could be making the data available the next time the program will run, or indeed when the computer is switched back on.

Physical design
When applied to a database essentially means converting a logical data model into structures that could be implemented on either a manual or specific computerised system.

Primary key
This relates to the column or columns that uniquely identify each row within a table.

QBE (query by example)
This is a method of devising a query based on interactive use of a grid table together with filters. It is a much more 'visual' approach to devising queries than the use of statements within a programming language such as SQL.

Query
This is a request instruction sent to a DBMS to retrieve data that matches the request sent.

Record
This is generally accepted as a single entry to a file but used by Microsoft to depict a row of information within a database table.

Recursive relationship
This is a relationship in which an entity is related to itself. The relation is said to be unary and not the normal binary relationship.

Referential integrity
These are the rules used within a DBMS to ensure the validity of data between tables. This contrasts with 'constraints' which apply within a column or table. Referential integrity ensures that a foreign key must either be associated with a primary key value within the database or be null.

Relation
This is just another term for a table within a database.

Relational database management system (RDBMS)
This is simply a database system based on the relational model of data.

Relational model
This is a database model comprising tables with relationships existing between the tables. This was originally proposed by E. F. Codd in the 1970s.

Relationship
In the context of an RDBMS, a relationship is an association between the different entities.

Repeating group
This describes the repeating of data within specific columns over several rows. Generally indicates the need for further optimisation to be carried out.

Requirements analysis
This is often a formal document identifying both the data that needs to be stored within a database as well as what has to be done to that data.

Restore
This describes the process of recovering a database from a backup copy held elsewhere.

Rollback
This is a process of sequentially reversing the latest entered transactions to a database to take it back to a previously defined state.

Row
This describes an entry in a relational table, an instance of data held in the table.

Schema
This describes the structure or organisation of a particular database system, often referred to as the database design.

Server
See *database server*.

Structured Query Language (SQL)
This is a non-procedural programming language used to define, manipulate and query data within a database. There are many different dialects of SQL but it still remains one of the most popular programming interfaces to a database.

Synonym
This refers to two different names used to describe the same thing and often causes confusion when constructing databases in that what one department may call an item, another department may call something different. An example would be Employee Number and Payroll Number.

Table
This is the basic data structure used within a relational database to represent a relational concept. Consists of columns (attributes) and rows (instances).

Transaction
This is a name given to a logical unit of work that must be completed as a whole or be rejected as a whole. It takes a database from one safe condition to another safe condition and is managed by the DBMS.

Tuple
This is the term used to describe a single row within a table, an instance of table data.

Union
A relational operator which, when applied to two tables containing the same structure, will combine the rows from both tables removing any redundant rows in the process.

Unique identifier
This is the name of any column or combination of columns whose value can uniquely identify a specific row within the table. This could be used as the primary key within the set of relations.

View
This is a virtual table or window created as a result of querying a database. It behaves like a table for as long as the view remains in existence.

XML
The is an abbreviation for Extensible Markup Language, a specification adopted by the Worldwide Web Consortium (W3C) as a standard for text format used especially for the transfer of information over the Web.

Index

access, restricting, 82
Access
  available data types, 54–5
  building a database, 57–71
  indexes, 56, 57
  SQL, 94–5
accountability, 81
ACID, 84, 140g
active data objects, 105
ad-hoc query, 140g
aggregate functions, 127, 140g
aliases, using, 120
ALTER TABLE, 91
alternate keys, 18
anomalies, normalisation, 48
ANSI-SPARC three layer architecture, 12, 13f
application domains, 7
application programming interfaces (API), 104, 140g
application software, 140g
arithmetic operations, on columns, 120
ASCII, 111, 140g
atomic values, 45, 46
atomicity, 84, 140g
attributes, 12, 30, 31f, 140g
authentication, 82, 140g
auto numbers, 53
availability, 85
Avg function, 127

B-tree, 55–7, 141g
backups, 85, 140–1g
batch processing, 141g
bit, 141g
built-in functions, 125–7
business integrity, 84
byte, 141g

candidate keys, 18, 141g
cardinality, 27, 37–40, 141g
Cartesian product, 130, 141g
cascading delete, 141g
cascading update, 141g
catalogue, 141g

category theory, 113
CIA security model approach, 84–5
circular wait condition, 87
client-server, 100–1, 141g
clustering, 142g
Codd, E.F., 5–6
collating sequence, 142g
columns, 7, 15
  arithmetic operations, 120
  defined, 142g
  formal name, 6
  selecting, 119
  using an alias, 120
combo boxes, 85
command differences, Oracle and Access, 95
command-line interface, 142g
commit, 142g
composite keys, 16, 142g
computer theft, 84–5
concatenation, 121
conceptual data models, 142g
conceptual level, three-layer architecture, 12
concurrency, 142g
concurrency control, 86–7, 101
concurrency errors, 83
confidentiality, 84
connectivity, 104–5
consistency, 83–4, 142g
consistent state, 83
constraint, 142g
cookies, 101–2
correlated sub-query, 142g
Count function, 127
CREATE TABLE, 91–2
crow's foot notation, 27
CRUD functions, 142g

damage, deliberate, 83
data
  defined, 142g
  saving, 2–3
  storage, 2, 3
data access objects, 104–5